WORKBOOK

AQA GCSE

ENGLISH

LANGUAGE

READING SKILLS
TARGETING
GRADES 6-9

Caroline Davis
Jo Heathcote
Emma Slater
Nicola Williams

OXFORD
UNIVERSITY PRESS

Great Clarendon Street, Oxford, OX2 6DP, United Kingdom

Oxford University Press is a department of the University of Oxford.
It furthers the University's objective of excellence in research, scholarship, and
education by publishing worldwide. Oxford is a registered trade mark of Oxford
University Press in the UK and in certain other countries

British Library Cataloguing in Publication Data

Data available

ISBN 978-0-19-843746-8

10 9 8 7 6 5 4 3 2 1

Printed in India by Multivista Global Pvt. Ltd.

Acknowledgements
The authors and publisher would like to thank the following for permission to use
photographs and other copyright material:

Cover: Panoramic Images/Getty Images. **p103:** © Thomas Dworzak/Magnum Photos.

Every effort has been made to contact copyright holders of material reproduced in
this book. Any omissions will be rectified in subsequent printings if notice is given
to the publisher.

The authors and publisher are grateful for permission to include the following
copyright material:

Candace Bushnell: *Lipstick Jungle* (Abacus, 2013), copyright © Candace Bushnell
2005, reprinted by permission of the Publishers, Little, Brown Book Group Ltd.

Frank Delaney: *Ireland: a novell* (Sphere, 2005), copyright © Frank Delaney 2005,
reprinted by permission of the Publishers, Little, Brown Book Group Ltd.

E M Forster: *A Room with a View* (Penguin Classics, 2012), first published by Edward
Arnold in 1909, reprinted by permission of The Provost and Scholars of King's
College. Cambridge and The Society of Authors as their Representative.

Khaled Hosseini: *A Thousand Splendid Suns* (Bloomsbury, 2008), copyright © Khyaled
Hosseini 2008, reprinted by permission of Bloomsbury Publishing Plc.

Caitlin Moran: *Moranifesto* (Ebury Books, 2016), copyright © Casa Bevron 2016,
reprinted by permission of The Random House Group Ltd.

Terry Pratchett: *Wyrd Sisters* (Victor Gollancz, 1988/Corgi, 2012), copyright
© Terry and Lyn Pratchett 1988, reprinted by permission of the publishers, the Orion
Publishing Group.

Jay Rayner: 'Riley's fish shack, Tynemouth: restaurant review', theguardian.com,
30 Oct 2016, copyright © Guardian News and Media Ltd 2016, 2019, reprinted
by permission of GNM.

Donna Tartt: *The Secret History* (Viking, 1992/Penguin, 1993, 2016), copyright
© Donna Tartt 1992, used by permission of Penguin Books Ltd.

Rosemary Waugh: 'Home futures', *Time Out* London, 5 Dec 2018, reprinted by
permission of the author and of Time Out England Ltd

Although we have made every effort to trace and contact all copyright holders before
publication this has not been possible in all cases. If notified, the publisher will
rectify any errors or omissions at the earliest opportunity.

Contents

Introduction

AQA GCSE English Language: specification overview

The grade you receive at the end of your AQA GCSE English Language course is entirely based on your performance in two exam papers. You will be assessed on your Reading Skills in Section A of each paper.

The following provides a summary of how you will be assessed.

Questions and marks	Assessment Objectives
Paper 1: Explorations in creative reading and writing Section A: Reading Exam text: ● One unseen literature fiction text Exam questions and marks: ● One short form question (1 x 4 marks) ● Two longer form questions (2 x 8 marks) ● One extended question (1 x 20 marks)	● AO1 ● AO2 ● AO4
Paper 2: Writers' viewpoints and perspectives Section A: Reading Exam text: ● One unseen non-fiction text and one unseen literary non-fiction text Exam questions and marks: ● One short form question (1 x 4 marks) ● Two longer form questions (1 x 8 marks and 1 x 12 marks) ● One extended question (1 x 16 marks)	● AO1 ● AO2 ● AO3

Assessment Objectives	
AO1	● Identify and interpret explicit and implicit information and ideas. ● Select and synthesise evidence from different texts.
AO2	Explain, comment on and analyse how writers use language and structure to achieve effects and influence readers, using relevant subject terminology to support their views.
AO3	Compare writers' ideas and perspectives, as well as how these are conveyed, across two or more texts.
AO4	Evaluate texts critically and support this with appropriate textual references.

How this workbook is structured

The workbook is split into four chapters and each chapter focuses on a specific reading skill, linking it closely to the exam questions where that skill is assessed.

- Chapter 1 explores the language writers use, looking at the 20th and 21st-century fiction texts and 19th-century non-fiction texts you will encounter in Papers 1 and 2.

- Chapter 2 focuses on how and why writers choose to **structure** texts in a particular way, and is based around the 20th and 21st-century fiction texts from Paper 1.

- Chapter 3 offers support for evaluating texts (Question 4 of Paper 1), identifying what the question is asking you to **evaluate** and write an evaluation.

- Chapter 4 moves on to comparisons of texts, focusing on the non-fiction texts in Paper 2 and again looking at what you are being asked to compare and how you write a comparison.

In each chapter you will find guidance on how to improve your reading skills, activities that build up to answering an exam-style question, accessible explanations of technical and literary terms, and extracts from sample student responses.

> **Key terms**
>
> **evaluate:** to assess something and understand its quality
>
> **structure:** (verb) organise the text, e.g. by including an introduction, headings, subheadings, lists, and grouping ideas into paragraphs

Sample exam papers

The workbook concludes with two full sample exam papers, one for Paper 1 and one for Paper 2.

What are the main features within this workbook?

Activities

To help you practise your reading responses, you will find activities through this workbook linked to the types of questions you will face in your exams. The source texts also reflect the types of texts you will be reading and responding to in your exams.

Upgrade

The Upgrade feature offers guidance to help with your exam preparation and performance.

Key terms and glossed words

These features help support your understanding of key terms and more difficult words within a source text. For ease of reference, there is also a complete list of key terms at the end of the workbook.

Progress check

At the end of each chapter you will find Progress checks. These enable you to use self-assessment to establish how confident you feel about what you have been learning and help you to identify areas for further practice.

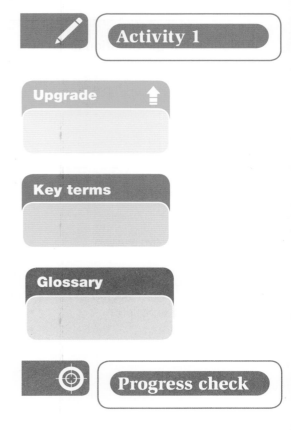

Activity 1

Upgrade

Key terms

Glossary

Progress check

Unit 1: Working with modern fiction texts (Paper 1 Question 2)

Understand it

Paper 1 Question 2 is a straightforward question asking you to make a detailed analysis of a range of the most interesting words and phrases that the writer has chosen. You should include sophisticated and accurate use of subject terminology. You will be given a short extract from the source material to work with.

Learning focus:
- Identify and select features of language.
- Analyse the writer's use of language to achieve effects in a modern fiction text.
- Use relevant and accurate subject terminology.

Activity 1

Take a look at how Question 2 will be phrased.

> **Example Exam Question**
>
> **2** Look in detail at this extract, from **lines x to x** of the source. (You will be given a specific section to look at within the extract.)
>
> How does the writer use language here to describe xxxxx? (A specific topic will be given.)
>
> You could include the writer's choice of:
>
> - words and phrases
>
> - language features and techniques
>
> - sentence forms.
>
> **[8 marks]**

Notice that the question asks 'how' not 'what'. What is the difference in asking 'how' the writer uses language rather than 'what' language is being used?

- -

- -

Upgrade

Spend only 10–15 minutes on Paper 1 Question 2. This does not include your reading time.

Take a look at the mark scheme for some help.

Level 4 Detailed, perceptive analysis **7–8 marks**	Shows detailed and perceptive understanding of language: • Analyses the effects of the writer's choices of language • Selects a judicious range of textual detail • Makes sophisticated and accurate use of subject terminology
Level 3 Clear, relevant explanation **5–6 marks**	Shows clear understanding of language: • Explains clearly the effects of the writer's choices of language • Selects a range of relevant textual detail • Makes clear and accurate use of subject terminology

Activity 2

The mark scheme shows that the key skill the examiner is looking for is your ability to comment on the effects of language devices. Look at the highlighted words. How is 'Detailed, perceptive analysis' different to 'Clear, relevant explanation'?

Think of the mark scheme as a ladder of skills. To secure Grades 6–9, you should be aiming for your work to hit the descriptors 'detailed' and 'perceptive'. This means your analysis needs to be thorough, thoughtful and developed.

So, the recipe for success at Grades 6–9 is to:

- thoughtfully select an appropriate word, phrase, collection of words or feature of language, using accurate subject terminology

- cover more than one feature of language and suggest more than one effect of each feature. This enables you to analyse layers of meaning

- write a developed analysis on the effects of these examples. Remember, this is the key skill being tested

- demonstrate accurate and deep understanding in order to be 'perceptive' for Level 4.

Before you start revising for this task, it's important to check your understanding of what the question demands:

	I'm confident	I need more practice	I'm not confident
Do I understand the difference between 'how' and 'what'?			
Do I understand what is meant by 'detailed' and 'perceptive'?			
Do I really know what a sophisticated analysis of the effects of language choices is?			

Upgrade

The key skill that is being assessed in this question is your ability to comment effectively on the *effects* of language choices. Your ability to do this is what determines the level you will be awarded. Being able to select relevant examples and use accurate subject terminology will support your analysis.

Upgrade

Level 4 asks for 'sophisticated' use of subject terminology. This means that you should explore **connotations** of language and offer layers of interpretation with subtle connections.

Key term

connotation: an idea or feeling suggested, in addition to the main meaning

Revise it

Activity 3

Carefully read the extract below twice. There will be some words you have not come across before. Use a dictionary to find the meanings of any unknown vocabulary in the extract.

Answer the following questions on separate paper as a starting point.

a. Highlight any repeated words. Why do you think these specific words are repeated?

b. Circle any words in the extract connected with sound. Some are examples of **onomatopoeia** because they sound similar to the noise they refer to. Other words are connected to sound by the use of **alliteration**, like 'feathers falling'. What impression of the scene do these words give you?

c. Underline any words in the extract connected with movement. Then highlight any of these words that are **verbs**. What impression of the scene do these verbs give you?

This extract is from *The Years*, a novel by English writer Virginia Woolf, published in 1937. It follows the fortunes of an upper-middle class family called the Pargiters, over a period of 57 years.

The Years by Virginia Woolf

It was January. Snow was falling; snow had fallen all day. The sky spread like a grey goose's wing from which feathers were falling all over England. The sky was nothing but a flurry of falling flakes. Lanes were levelled; hollows filled; the snow clogged the streams;
5   obscured windows, and lay wedged against doors. There was a faint murmur in the air, a slight **crepitation**, as if the air itself were turning to snow; otherwise all was silent, save when a sheep coughed, snow flopped from a branch, or slipped in an avalanche down some roof in London. Now and again a shaft of light spread
10 slowly across the sky as a car drove through the muffled roads. But as the night wore on, snow covered the wheel ruts; softened to nothingness the marks of the traffic, and coated monuments, palaces and statues with a thick vestment of snow.

It was still snowing when the young man came from the House
15 Agents to see over Abercorn Terrace. The snow cast a hard white glare upon the walls of the bathroom, showed up the cracks on the enamel bath, and the stains on the wall. Eleanor stood looking out of the window. The trees in the back garden were heavily lined with snow; all the roofs were softly moulded with snow; it was
20 still falling. She turned. The young man turned too. The light was unbecoming to them both, yet the snow – she saw it through the window at the end of the passage – was beautiful, falling.

Key terms

alliteration: when the same letter or sound occurs at the beginning of neighbouring words

connective: a word that joins phrases or sentences, such as *moreover*, *as a result*, *furthermore*, *in addition*, *not only… but also*, *because, therefore, consequently*

fricative: repetition of the consonants 'f', 'v' and 'th'

onomatopoeia: the use of words that imitate or suggest what they stand for, e.g. *cuckoo, plop*

simile: a comparison showing the similarity between two different things, stating that one is like the other

verb: a word that presents a movement, an action or a feeling, and tells us about when it happened

Glossary

crepitation: a crackling or rattling sound

Remember that different readers may have different impressions of a scene, so you should offer more than one interpretation for a higher mark. For example, the alliteration of 'feathers falling' creates a softness linked with the feeling of snowflakes on the skin. It also uses a **fricative**, which emphasises the soft sound as snow falls. You could use **connectives** such as 'alternatively', 'conversely' and 'on the other hand' to structure your analysis.

You won't earn marks by just identifying language features and using subject terminology. You have to be able to analyse in detail the language that the writer has chosen, to show your deep understanding of its effects. Therefore, you need to select details from the text carefully so that you can write an insightful and developed analysis.

Upgrade

When you have identified a range of language and features in a text, begin your analysis with a feature you can write about in detail.

Activity 4

The extract on the exam paper will have been chosen because it contains a range of language features. For example, you could start your analysis with the two **similes** below. Complete the table, then highlight the simile you could write about in the most detail. This is the feature you would start your response with.

Simile	The effects and why the writer may have chosen this
'The sky spread like a grey goose's wing from which feathers were falling all over England'	
'a slight crepitation, as if the air itself were turning to snow'	

Activity 5

The mark scheme for Question 2 asks for 'perceptive and detailed understanding of language'. To demonstrate this, you need to be able to analyse a wide range of language features, though they will not *all* be in the extract.

a. Draw a line from each language feature in the table below to the correct definition.

Language feature	Definition
alliteration	repetition of a consonant sound in words close to one another
assonance	repetition of the same letter or sound at the start of words close to one another
consonance	repetition of the consonants 'f', 'v' and 'th'
fricative	repetition of soft consonant sounds, such as 's', to create a hissing, hushing or whooshing noise
sibilance	repetition of a vowel sound in words close to one another

b. Write an example below of alliteration, assonance, consonance and sibilance from the extract on page 8.

Alliteration: _____

_____

Assonance: _____

_____

Consonance: _____

_____

Sibilance: _____

_____

Activity 6

a. Read the three student responses below. Rank them according to the quality of their analysis, from the best to the least successful.

Student 1

The writer uses alliteration to make the snow sound soft: 'a flurry of falling flakes'. In addition, the writer uses sibilance, which is when the 's' sound is repeated: 'softened to nothingness'. There is also consonance in the line, 'lanes were levelled; hollows filled'. All these language features emphasise the snow being soft.

Activity 6 *continued*

Student 2

The writer uses alliteration of the fricative sound 'f' in the phrase, 'a flurry of falling flakes'. This creates an airy sound, which is gentle and soothing, suggesting the softness of the snow and creating an atmosphere of quietness and peace. This is followed by consonance in 'lanes were levelled; hollows filled', which continues the feeling of relaxation. Alternatively, the repetition of these smooth consonants, both within and at the start of words, creates a flow of soft sound, suggesting that the snow has a hypnotic effect.

Student 3

The writer uses a variety of language features such as sibilance of the letter 's' and the fricative 'f' sound to recreate the sounds and feelings of snowfall. This has a mesmerising effect on the reader, who is relaxed by the description of the sound of the falling snow. Use of assonance and consonance develops this further, allowing the reader to lose themselves in the description.

b. Look again at the two responses you did not rank first. On a separate piece of paper, write advice for each student to enable them to improve the quality of their analysis and increase their mark.

Key terms

assonance: repetition of a vowel sound in words close to one another

consonance: repetition of a consonant sound in words close to one another

sibilance: repetition of soft consonant sounds, such as 's', to create a hissing, hushing or whooshing noise

Try it with support

Read the following extract through carefully twice. It is the opening to the fantasy novel *Wyrd Sisters* by Terry Pratchett, published in 1988. It is part of his Discworld series and features the three witches Granny Weatherwax, Nanny Ogg and Magrat Garlick. Look up the meanings of any words you don't know.

Wyrd Sisters by Terry Pratchett

The wind howled. Lightning stabbed at the earth erratically, like an inefficient assassin. Thunder rolled back and forth across the dark, rain-lashed hills. The night was as black as the inside of a cat. It was the kind of night, you could believe, on which gods
5 moved men as though they were pawns on the chessboard of fate. In the middle of this elemental storm a fire gleamed among the dripping **furze** bushes like the madness in a weasel's eye. It illuminated three hunched figures. As the cauldron bubbled an **eldritch** voice shrieked: "When shall we three meet again?" There
10 was a pause. Finally another voice said, in far more ordinary tones: "Well, I can do next Tuesday."

Glossary

furze: a type of spiky, thorny bush

eldritch: weird and sinister or ghostly

Activity 7

a. Where is this opening set and how do you know?

----

b. How does the writer show that this is a fantasy genre?

----

c. Label any features of language that you recognise on the extract on page 11. Use your work from the 'Revise it' section on pages 8–11 to help you.
For example, look at how the weather is **personified** with human actions and emotions to create a specific atmosphere and feeling. This is called **pathetic fallacy**.

d. Find the four similes in this extract, then complete the table below to analyse their effects. The first one has been done for you as an example.

Simile	Effects
'Lightning stabbed at the earth erratically, <u>like</u> an inefficient assassin.'	Personifies the weather (pathetic fallacy); uses violent verb 'stabbed', but the adverb 'erratically' suggests not hitting target; therefore described as potentially lethal though unsuccessful at present.

Activity 7 *continued*

e. In the exam, you would not have time or need to write about all four similes in order to demonstrate the range required for the highest marks. So select one simile you could analyse in the most detail and depth. How does the writer use this simile to help set the scene?

----

f. Look back at the language features you labelled in Activity 7c. Choose the four you would write about in a full response. You should select four language features that enable you to analyse perceptively and write a response of the highest quality.

Activity 8

Now write a response to the following example Paper 1 Question 2. Use a separate piece of paper.

Example Exam Question

2 Look in detail at this extract, from **lines 1 to 11** of the source.

(The source is from *Wyrd Sisters* by Terry Pratchett, as appears on page 11.)

How does the writer use language here to describe the weather?

You could include the writer's choice of:

- words and phrases
- language features and techniques
- sentence forms.

[8 marks]

You could use some of these phrases to structure your response:

- The writer's purpose…
- The personification and onomatopoeia in the short sentence, 'The wind howled', creates…
- … as though the weather is an enemy…
- … suggests a higher power…
- … reflects the sound of…

Upgrade

Offer more than one **interpretation** of the chosen simile and, if the simile demonstrates other language features too, you can also analyse these.

Key terms

interpret: explain the meaning of something in your own words, showing your understanding

pathetic fallacy: giving human feelings to things or animals

personification: giving human qualities or emotions to something that is not human

Unit 2: Working with 19th-century non-fiction texts (Paper 2 Question 3)

Understand it

Paper 2 Question 3 asks you to analyse language features in non-fiction source material. However, the selected part of the extract is not printed separately as it is for Paper 1 Question 2. Instead, you need to find and re-read the specified lines in the whole extract before you start your analysis. In addition, you may be asked to analyse language in the 19th-century text in Paper 2, whereas the text in Paper 1 will be 20th or 21st century.

Read the extract below carefully twice. It is taken from a collection of accounts about balloon travel, mainly over England and France, published in 1863. The author, James Glashier, was one of the aeronauts. There may be some words you have not come across before, so use a dictionary to find the meanings of any new vocabulary.

Travels in the Air by James Glashier

Towns and cities, when viewed from the balloon are like models in motion. I shall always remember the ascent of 9th October, 1863, when we passed over London about sunset. At the time when we were 7,000 feet high, and directly over London Bridge,
5   the scene around was one that cannot probably be equalled in the world. We were still so low as not to have lost sight of the details of the spectacle which presented itself to our eyes; and with one glance the homes of 3,000,000 people could be seen, and so distinct was the view, that every large building was easily
10   distinguishable. In fact, the whole of London was visible, and some parts most clearly. All round, the suburbs were also very distinct, with their lines of detached villas, imbedded as it were in a mass of shrubs; beyond, the country was like a garden, its fields, well-marked, becoming smaller and smaller as the
15   eye wandered farther and farther away. Again looking down, there was the Thames, throughout its whole length, without the slightest mist, dotted over its winding course with innumerable ships and steamboats, like moving toys. Gravesend was visible, also the mouth of the Thames, and the coast around as far as
20   Norfolk. The southern shore of the mouth of the Thames was not so clear, but the sea beyond was seen for many miles; when at a higher elevation, I looked for the coast of France, but was unable to see it. On looking round, the eye was arrested by the garden-like appearance of the county of Kent, till again London claimed
25   yet more careful attention.

Upgrade

You should spend 12–18 minutes on Paper 2 Question 3. This does not include your reading time.

Smoke, thin and blue, was curling from it, and slowly moving away in beautiful curves, from all except one part, south of the Thames, where it was less blue and seemed more dense, till the cause became evident; it was mixed with mist rising from the

30 ground, the southern limit of which was bounded by an even line, doubtless indicating the meeting of the **subsoils** of gravel and clay. The whole scene was surmounted by a canopy of blue, everywhere free from cloud, except near the horizon, where a band of **cumulus and stratus** extended all round, forming a

35 fitting boundary to such a glorious view.

As seen from the earth, the sunset this evening was described as fine, the air being clear and the shadows well defined; but, as we rose to view it and its effects, the golden hues increased in intensity; their richness decreased as the distance from the sun

40 increased, both right and left; but still as far as 90° from the sun, rose-coloured clouds extended. The remainder of the circle was completed, for the most part, by pure white cumulus of well-rounded and symmetrical forms.

I have seen London by night. I have crossed it during the day at

45 the height of four miles. I have often admired the splendour of sky scenery, but never have I seen anything which surpassed this spectacle. The roar of the town heard at this elevation was a deep, rich, continuous sound—the voice of labour. At four miles above London, all was hushed; no sound reached our ears.

Glossary

subsoils: the soil that is just under the surface of the ground

cumulus and stratus: types of cloud

Now take a look at the specific instructions for this question.

Example Exam Question

3 You now need to refer **only** to Source B from **lines 26 to 49**.

The question clearly indicates the part of Source B you should focus your response on. Draw a line across the text at line 26 and again at line 49 to separate this section from the whole text. You should always do this as responses referring to lines not specified in the question will *not* be rewarded, however good they are.

Activity 1

Now look at the specific focus of the question.

Example Exam Question

> **3** How does the writer use language to describe the view of London?

a. Highlight the words in the question that indicate the purpose or focus of the language features you have to comment on.

b. Use this information to label any language features in the extract that are relevant to the question. Don't label anything that is not relevant, as you will not be rewarded for this.

Underneath the question, there will be bullet points to help guide you in your response.

Example Exam Question

You could include the writer's choice of:

- words and phrases
- language features and techniques
- sentence forms.

Activity 2

Look closely at the last bullet point in the question above. Identify any sentence forms that are relevant to the focus of the question.

The guiding bullet points for Paper 1 Question 3 (on **structure**) also suggest considering sentence forms. So you need to understand how sentence forms can be analysed in different ways to meet the requirements of the structure question on Paper 1 and the language questions on both papers. This is outlined below:

Paper 1, Question 2 and Paper 2, Question 3 on the writer's use of language	Paper 1, Question 3 on the writer's use of structure
You need to focus on: - one particular sentence - how it is constructed at sentence level, e.g. its length and complexity - its purpose, e.g. as an exclamation, statement, interrogative, imperative or question - the significance of the content and meaning of the sentence - any linguistic devices in the sentence.	You need to focus on: - one particular sentence, at whole text level - its significance at that specific position in the whole text - its purpose in the text as a whole.

Upgrade

Notice that Paper 1 Question 3 states '*could* include' and not '*should* include'. This indicates that the bullet points are only a guide and you do not have to write about each bullet point. You are free to include your own choice of material from the specified section, but you must ensure that you choose language features and that those you choose are relevant to the stated question focus.

Key term

structure: (noun) the organisation of a text

Activity 3

Read the two student responses below. They both analyse sentence forms, based on the same quotation.

Student 1

The sentence, 'At four miles above London, all was hushed; no sound reached our ears' is important because it links back to the location above the earth that was established earlier. The position of this sentence at the end of the extract summarises the change from the noise at ground level to the silence up in the air, with the semi-colon enabling the writer to juxtapose sound with silence.

Student 2

The sentence, 'At four miles above London, all was hushed; no sound reached our ears' is important because it reflects the contrast of silence in the air with noise at ground level. This is emphasised through sibilance of the 's' and onomatopoeia of 'hushed', where the reader experiences the sound themselves and so truly feels the effect of the silence. This sentence is important because it emphasises how high the balloon is.

a. Identify which response is analysing structure and which is analysing language.

----

b. Look at the short sentence, 'I have seen London by night' on line 44 of the extract. Why do you think the writer has chosen to use a short sentence for this statement?

Revise it

The extract below is a description by Charles Dickens of the Covent
Garden markets in London in 1879. Read it through carefully twice,
looking up any vocabulary that you are unfamiliar with.

> ### *Dickens's Dictionary of London* by Charles Dickens
>
> Covent Garden – No visitor to London should miss paying at
> least two visits to Covent-garden: one at early morning. Say at
> 6 am – the hour is an untimely one, but no one will regret the
> effort that the early rising involves – to see the vegetable market;
> 5 the other, later on, to see the fruits and flowers. All night long on
> the great main roads the rumble of the heavy waggons seldom
> ceases, and before daylight the 'market' is crowded. The very
> loading of these waggons is in itself a wonder, and the wall-
> like regularity with which cabbages, cauliflowers, turnips, are
> 10 built up to a height of some 12ft. is nothing short of marvellous.
> Between 5 and 6 o'clock the light traps of the green-grocers of
> the metropolis rattle up, and all the streets around the market
> become thronged with their carts, while the **costermongers**
> come in in immense numbers. By 6 o'clock the market is fairly
> 15 open, and the din and bustle are surprising indeed. Gradually
> the large piles of vegetables melt away. If it be summer-time
> flowers as well as fruits are sold at the early markets. Then there
> are hundreds of women and girls among the crowd, purchasing
> bunches of roses, violets, and other flowers, and then sitting
> 20 down on the steps of the church, or of the houses round the
> market, dividing the large bunches into smaller ones, or making
> those pretty button-hole bouquets in which our London flower-
> girls can now fairly hold their own in point of taste with those of
> France or Italy. Even in winter flower-girls find materials for their
> 25 little bouquets; for, thanks to steam, violets are brought from the
> Scilly and Channel Isles, and even from the South of France,
> and there is always a certain supply of hothouse flowers; so that
> there are many flower-girls who ply their trade at all seasons of
> the year. After 8 o'clock the market becomes quiet. The great
> 30 waggons have moved off; the debris of cabbage-leaves and
> other vegetable matter has been swept up, and Covent-garden
> assumes its everyday aspect. And a very pretty aspect it is. The
> avenue as at all times of the year a sight, the shops competing
> with each other in a display of flowers and fruit such as can
> 35 scarcely, if at all, be rivalled in any capital of Europe. In winter the
> aspect of the fruit shops changes somewhat, but not so much
> as might have been expected, for steam and heat have made it
> possible for the rich to eat many fruits, which formerly were in
> season but a month or two, all the year round. On each side of

40 the main avenue are enclosed squares, and here the wholesale fruit market is carried on. In winter there are thousands of boxes of oranges, hundreds of sacks of nuts, boxes of Hamburg grapes and of French winter pears, barrels of bright American apples. At ten o'clock the sale begins; auctioneers stand on boxes, and
45 while the more expensive fruits are purchased by the West-end fruiterers, the cheaper are briskly bid for by the costermonger. Listen to the prices at which the fruit sells, and you will wonder no longer at the marvellous bargains at which these **itinerant vendors** are able to retail their fruits, although, perhaps, you may
50 be astonished when you remember the prices at which you have seen the contents of some of these boxes marked in fruiterers' shops. Outside the market there is almost always something to see. In winter **a score** of men are opening orange boxes and sorting their contents; in autumn dozens of women and girls are
55 extracting walnuts from juicy green outside cases; in spring-time the side facing the church is occupied by dealers in spring and bedding flowers, and the pavement is aglow with colour of flower and leaf, and in the early summer hundreds of women and girls are busily occupied in shelling peas. Country visitors will go away
60 from Covent Garden with the conviction that to see flowers and fruits in perfection it is necessary to come to London.

Glossary

costermonger: a person selling fruit/vegetables from a hand cart in the street
vendor: seller

itinerant: a person who travels from place to place
a score: 20

Juxtaposition is when writers place together or describe ideas, objects or images that are not similar so that the differences between them are emphasised.

Activity 4

Read lines 1–5 again. The writer juxtaposes time by referring to '6 am' and how the hour is 'untimely' in order to contrast this with the scene 'later on'. This is further emphasised by the repetition of the **adverb** 'early'. The reader knows that a description of how the scene changes to a busy marketplace will follow and anticipates this.

a. Read lines 9–20. What two aspects is the writer contrasting here?

Key terms

adverb: a word used to describe verbs, adjectives or other adverbs

juxtaposition: when things are put next to each other or close together to contrast them

Activity 4 *continued*

b. What is the effect of the juxtaposition this time?

----

c. What is juxtaposed in lines 24–38 and what is its effect? Think in terms of the passing of time.

Upgrade

When explaining the effect of juxtaposition, consider whether the writer wants to surprise the reader, create suspense, add vividness to an image or help the reader understand one thing through comparison to another.

Activity 5

A **semantic field** is a set of words that refer to a specific subject. They are related to one another through their meanings. In the extract, there are various semantic fields.

a. Complete the table below by placing words from the extract in each category. Some words have been added to start you off and the last column is blank for you to add another category.

People	Goods sold	Time	Places	
Flower-girls	Roses			

b. What is the effect of each of the semantic fields that Dickens creates? Write a paragraph on a separate piece of paper.

Upgrade

Some reasons writers use semantic fields could be:

- to keep a certain image in the reader's mind
- to reflect the writer's interests
- to emphasise an image, idea, character, place, etc.
- to create a specific atmosphere
- to emphasise the writer's use of other language features.

You should always give details of what the image, interest, idea or atmosphere is.

Key term

semantic field:
a collection of words with similar meanings or relevant to the same theme

Activity 6

a. Dickens' combination of juxtaposition and semantic fields enables him to create the atmosphere of a marketplace that becomes progressively busier. Annotate the extract with any other language techniques that Dickens uses to do this.

b. How much time should you spend on Paper 2 Question 3 in the exam?

- -

c. How does Dickens use language to create the atmosphere of a busy marketplace? Write a full response on a separate piece of paper. Time yourself and ensure you do not go beyond the recommended time.

Upgrade

If you can't recall how long to spend on this question, look back at the 'Understand it' section on page 14.

Try it with support

Read the letter below carefully twice, finding the meanings of any unfamiliar words.

In this letter of 1851, the writer, Charlotte Brontë, describes to her father her second visit to the Great Exhibition in the Crystal Palace in London. The Great Exhibition was visited by millions of people, who would have seen inventions and manufactured goods from Britain as well as from other countries.

Letter from Charlotte Brontë to her father

Dear Papa, – I was very glad to hear that you continued in pretty good health, and that Mr. Cartman came to help you on Sunday. I fear you will not have had a very comfortable week in the dining-room; but by this time I suppose the parlour reformation
5   will be nearly completed, and you will soon be able to return to your own quarters. The letter you sent me this morning was from Mary Taylor. She continues well and happy in New Zealand, and her shop seems to answer well. The French newspaper duly arrived. Yesterday I went for the second time to the Crystal
10 Palace. We remained in it about three hours, and I must say I was more struck with it on this occasion than at my first visit, it is a wonderful place – vast, strange, new, and impossible to describe. Its grandeur does not consist in *one* thing, but in the assemblage of *all* things. Whatever human industry has created,
15 you find there, from the great compartments filled with railway engines and boilers, with mill machinery in full work, with splendid carriages of all kinds, with harness of every description – to the glass covered and velvet spread stands loaded with the most gorgeous work of the **goldsmith and silversmith**, and the
20 carefully guarded caskets full of real diamonds, and pearls worth hundreds of thousands of pounds. It may be called a **bazaar** or a fair, but it is such a bazaar or fair as Eastern **genii** might have created. It seems as if only magic could have gathered this mass of wealth from all ends of the earth – as if none but supernatural
25 hands could have arranged this, with such blaze and contrast of colours and marvellous power of effect. The multitude filling the great aisles seems ruled and subdued by some invisible influence. Amongst the thirty thousand souls that peopled it the day I was there not one loud noise was to be heard, not one
30 irregular movement seen; the living tide rolls on quietly, with a deep hum like the sea heard from the distance.

Mr. Thackeray is in high spirits about the success of his lectures. It is likely to add largely both to his fame and purse. He has, however, deferred this week's lecture till next Thursday, at the
35 earliest petition of the **duchesses and marchionesses**, who, on the day it should have been delivered, were necessitated to go down with the Queen and Court to Ascot Races. I told him I thought he did wrong to put off on their account – and I think so still. The amateur performance of Bulwer's play for the
40 Guild of Literature has likewise been deferred on account of the

races. I hope, dear papa, that you, Mr. Nicholls, and all at home continue well. Tell Martha to take her scrubbing and cleaning in moderation and not overwork herself. With kind regards to her and Tabby, – I am, your affectionate daughter,

45 C Brontë.

Glossary

goldsmith and silversmith: craftspeople who work with gold and silver

bazaar: market

genii: plural of genie; a supernatural being from Arabian folklore, often trapped in a bottle or oil lamp, who can grant wishes

duchesses and marchionesses: a duchess is married to a duke while a marchioness is married to a marquess, high-ranking members of the aristocracy

Activity 7

a. Mark off lines 9–28 on the extract. Find and label the **anaphora** in the first half of this section.

b. What is the effect of the anaphora?

Activity 8

A **noun phrase** is a group of words in a sentence that work in the same way as a **noun** but give more information about that noun. For example, 'carefully guarded caskets' is a noun phrase. Look at it in more detail:

> 'the carefully guarded caskets full of real diamonds, and pearls worth hundreds and thousands of pounds'

Notice the nouns in orange and how the words in green give additional information about those nouns, forming noun phrases.

Upgrade

Anaphora can persuade, add rhythm, intensify a meaning, add an emotion or make a point memorable. It may also, of course, have other effects.

Key terms

anaphora: the deliberate repetition of the first part of a sentence or phrase

noun: a noun identifies a person, place or thing

noun phrase: one or more adjectives with a noun, e.g. *clear + starry + night*

Activity 8 *continued*

a. Complete the table below to analyse the words that form the noun phrases.

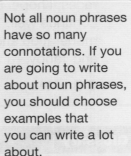

Words that form the noun phrase	What these words suggest
'carefully guarded'	• The adverb 'carefully' suggests that the guards are attentive, cautious, watchful. • The verb 'guarded' suggests that the caskets are precious and attractive to thieves, and so require protection.
'real'	
'worth hundreds and thousands'	

b. Rank the noun phrases in the table from 1 to 3, according to how relevant you think they would be in a response on language features.

c. Label any other noun phrases in lines 9–28. Create a second table on separate paper to explore their connotations.

Activity 9

Remind yourself of how Paper 2 Question 3 will be phrased:

Example Exam Question

3 You now need to refer only to **lines 9 to 28**.

How does the writer use language to describe the Crystal Palace?

[12 marks]

Activity 9 *continued*

a. Highlight or underline any sentences that describe the Crystal Palace. This will ensure your focus is on the question.

b. Label any features of language that you have not yet identified. You may find onomatopoeia, for example.

c. Choose four aspects of language to write about in your response.

d. Write your timed response to the example exam question on page 24 on a separate piece of paper. Use your responses to previous activities in this unit as a starting point.

Upgrade

The quality of your response is important. In order to reach the higher marks, be selective and only choose language features that give you the opportunity to analyse in depth.

Progress check

	I'm confident	I need more practice	I'm not confident
I can identify which part of the full extract I need to focus my response on.			
I understand the language question and can identify the specific focus.			
I can identify, select and analyse a range of sentence forms in a language question.			
I can identify, select and analyse a range of language features in a language question, including:			
• alliteration			
• assonance			
• consonance			
• fricatives			
• onomatopoeia			
• sibilance			
• simile			
• verbs.			
I can analyse in depth and with sophistication.			

Unit 1: Understanding structural features (Paper 1 Question 3)

Understand it

Paper 1 Question 3 asks you to make a detailed analysis of the structural features the writer has chosen. You should include a range of well-chosen examples, while using accurate and sophisticated subject terminology.

Take a look at how Paper 1 Question 3 will be phrased.

Learning focus:

- Understand the differences between language features and structural features.
- Use terminology accurately.
- Differentiate between structure at whole text, paragraph and sentence level.

Example Exam Question

3   You now need to think about the **whole** of the source.

This text is from xxxxx. (You will be told if it is from the beginning, middle or ending of a novel or short story.)

How has the writer structured the text to interest you as a reader?

You could write about:

- what the writer focuses your attention on at the (beginning/ middle/end) of the source
- how and why the writer changes this focus as the source develops.
- any other structural features that interest you.

[8 marks]

Upgrade

Spend 10–12 minutes on Paper 1 Question 3. This does not include your reading time.

Notice that the question asks '*How* has the writer structured the text' not '*What* has the writer done to structure the text'. Whereas 'what' asks you to just identify the structural features being used, 'how' asks you to analyse the effects of that feature and explain its purpose in the text.

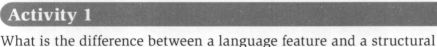

Activity 1

What is the difference between a language feature and a structural feature?

- -

- -

Now take a look at the mark scheme for this question. Think of the mark scheme as a ladder of skills. To secure Grades 6–9, you need to move from 'clear and relevant' to 'detailed and perceptive'. This means your analysis needs to be in-depth, thoughtful and extended.

Level 4 Detailed, perceptive analysis **7–8 marks**	Shows detailed and perceptive understanding of structural features: • Analyses the effects of the writer's choice of structural features • Selects a judicious range of examples • Makes sophisticated and accurate use of subject terminology
Level 3 Clear, relevant explanation **5–6 marks**	Shows clear understanding of structural features: • Explains clearly the effects of the writer's choice of structural features • Selects a range of relevant examples • Makes clear and accurate use of subject terminology

Activity 2

a. What are the differences in the mark schemes for Levels 3 and 4 for this question?

----

b. The mark scheme shows the skills needed to earn Grades 6–9. Look at the highlighted words. How is 'analyses' different to 'explains'?

----

c. Level 4 asks for a 'judicious' range of examples. What exactly does that mean?

----

d. How is 'a judicious range of examples' in Level 4 different to 'a range of relevant examples' in Level 3?

So, the recipe for success at Grades 6–9 is to:

• thoughtfully select an appropriate feature of structure, using accurate subject terminology

• give a carefully selected example or examples of the structural feature from the text. This may be in the form of a quotation, although sometimes quotations are not appropriate for describing structural features because they are too long and not selective enough

• write a developed analysis on the effect of these examples. You should aim to analyse three or four separate structural features. Remember, this is the key skill being tested

• demonstrate accurate and deep understanding in order to be 'perceptive' for Level 4.

Before you start revising for this task, it's important to check your understanding of what the question demands:

	I'm confident	I need more practice	I'm not confident
Do I understand the difference between language and structure?			
Do I understand what is meant by 'judicious'?			
Can I name and analyse a range of structural features?			

Revise it

Activity 3

The list of structural features below does not contain every structural device but it is a good starting point. Put each structural feature into the correct category in the table.

beginning   ending   change of topic   **temporal connective**

big to small picture   **flashback**   narrative voice   **motif**

foreshadowing   introduction of character   speech

setting   **topic sentence**   climax

Whole-text level	Paragraph level	Sentence level

Upgrade

A perceptive response needs to analyse structure in a more abstract way. This could include referring to concepts such as culture, race, class, age, time, space and history rather than just considering how a text opens, develops and closes.

Key terms

cohesive devices: techniques for connecting points, avoiding repetition and signposting arguments

flashback: a scene that returns to events in the past

foreshadowing: a sign or hint of something that will happen in the future

metaphor: a comparison showing the similarity between two quite different things, stating that one actually is the other

motif: a physical or metaphorical item that recurs in a text, taking on a range of meanings

Activity 4

a. Read the list of writing features below. Then put each feature into the correct category in the table. You may need to look up the meaning of some of the terms.

metaphor   beginning   **narrative perspective**   flashback

sibilance   assonance   topic sentence   temporal connective

simile   onomatopoeia   motif   list   sentence length

cliffhanger   flash-forward

Structural features	Language features

b. Highlight the terms you think are more sophisticated and would enable you to reach Level 4. Add any more structural terms you know to the table.

c. The structural features above are not the only ones. There are many that come into a range of categories. For example, narrative perspective and topic sentence are part of the narrative focus of a text, while temporal connectives are **cohesive devices** as they contribute to the way words, sentences and paragraphs link together to make a text flow. Which structural devices above relate to time shifts?

Key terms

narrative perspective: features that determine what is told and how in a story, including the narrator and/ or the character from whose point of view the story is told

narrative voice: the characteristic ways in which the narrator speaks and thinks

setting: the place or surroundings where an event takes place or something is positioned

temporal connective: a word or phrase that tells you when something is happening

topic sentence: the sentence that introduces or summarises the main idea in a paragraph

Read the extract below carefully twice. It is taken from the novel *The Last Days of Ojukwu* by Christopher Walker, published in 1976. It is set in Japan in the first half of the 20th century.

The Last Days of Ojukwu by Christopher Walker

Ojukwu went on over the ridge and down to the paddy fields. He waded knee deep in the brown mud and worked all day with the other old men and women and the young girls and boys. By evening, half the rice crop had been transplanted. That night

5   it rained without once stopping and Ojukwu was glad that he had not gone back to the city but had stayed with his old friend Tanato in his little farmhouse overlooking the rice fields. It rained all morning as they worked in the fields, but at noon the clouds departed and the sun beat down, but the tender shoots were

10 deep and safe under the brown water in the paddies. It was a pity that the sun came out, for otherwise Ojukwu might not have resisted his friend's invitation to stay yet another night. And who knows? He might have lived.

But Ojukwu trudged wearily back in the bright sun over the ridge

15 to the town. His son was due for leave and he might even be home for the feast. If he did come, how proud Ojukwu would be, for had not the Sun [*sic*] of God himself honoured him as a brave flier of the Empire, and how smart he would look in his pilot's uniform with his ribbons and medals, and especially the winged star for

20 supreme bravery of the Imperial Air Force. Who knows? That plane, which even now he could hear but not see, so high was it, might be bringing home his son, circling above the town ready to glide home to the airfield which lay in the next valley. And so Ojukwu topped the ridge and walked some yards down towards

25 the city and sat down by the side of the road, partly to regain his breath and partly to admire the view. That was the last time Ojukwu saw the city and the last thing but one he ever did see.

Activity 5

a. Make notes on the following questions.

Where is the action taking place?	
What is happening?	
Who is involved?	
What are you told about them?	
What is likely to come next?	

b. Label any structural features in the extract that you recognise. Use your work from Activities 3 and 4 to help you. For example, you could look for temporal connectives like 'that night'.

c. Look at the structural features below. They can all be found in the extract. Match each quotation to the correct feature.

Quotation	Structural feature
'Ojukwu went on over the ridge'	temporal connective
'He waded knee deep'	introduction of a character
'He might have lived.'	narrative perspective (third person)
'By evening, half the rice crop'	cliffhanger

A **discourse marker** is a signpost that links a sentence to what has already been written or what is going to come next and it can suggest the writer's attitude. Often a discourse marker will come at the start of a sentence or paragraph. For example, 'because' links cause and effect.

Activity 6

a. Read the extract on page 30 again. Then highlight the following discourse markers: by, but, as, otherwise, if, and, so.

b. Put each discourse marker into one of the categories below, depending on its purpose in the text.

Links to a previous sentence	Links with what will come next	Suggests the writer's attitude

Try it with support

Finding and naming the structural features the writer uses is not enough. The mark scheme asks you to show 'detailed and perceptive understanding' to achieve the highest marks, which means you must avoid vague generalisations such as:

> It makes the reader want to read on.

> It paints a picture in the reader's head.

Read the following extract from a student's response, which explains one of the structural features in the extract.

> The writer uses a cliffhanger, 'He might have lived.' This comes at the end, so the reader wants to find out what happened to Ojukwu and it puts them on the edge of their seat.

Upgrade

Your ideas must be supported by **evidence** from the text, whether it is **explicit** or **implicit**. Implicit evidence relies on you explaining the feature in your own words, whereas **explicit** evidence could be a short quotation.

Activity 7

a. Why would this response not achieve Level 3 in the mark scheme?

----

b. Rewrite the response, including the key phrases below.

> the position of this phrase is significant because
>
> the writer's purpose in positioning it here
>
> the position of the **modal verb** 'might' creates a feeling of
>
> hints at a follow-up   a plot device   introduces a conflict

----

----

c. Now, on separate paper, complete a full analysis of the other three structural features listed in Activity 5c.

Key terms

evidence: quotation or direct reference to the text

explicit: stating something openly and exactly

implicit: not directly stated in the text, but where the meaning is suggested by the information you are given and needs to be inferred or deduced

modal verb: a type of verb that goes before the main verb, e.g. *will, could, might, should, may, ought*

Activity 8

The final lines of the whole story read:

> But Ojukwu had died while the cloud still grew. He shrivelled up in the first wave of radiation – he and 100,000 others in Hiroshima died that day.

a. What do you learn in this final part of the story?

----

b. Why do you think the writer saves this vital information until the end?

33

Activity 9

Look back at the discourse markers you identified in Activity 6.

a. What did you notice about the use of 'otherwise' near the end of the extract?

----

b. How is the reader left feeling after this sentence?

----

c. How might these feelings change if this discourse marker was used at the start of the extract instead?

----

d. How does this discourse marker link to the two short sentences that follow it?

Upgrade

Considering your responses to analytical questions like these will help you to write a perceptive analysis of structure and aim towards the highest marks in this question.

Activity 10

Look at the writer's use of the discourse marker 'but', which occurs six times in the text. What questions do you need to ask yourself before you start writing your analysis of the use of this discourse marker?

a. --

----

b. --

----

c. --

----

d. --

Activity 11

Using your notes on the extract, improve the weak student response below. Make sure you ask yourself probing questions in order to demonstrate the detailed and perceptive understanding required for the higher marks.

Remember that structural features can be at whole-text level (e.g. beginnings, endings), at paragraph level (e.g. shifts in time, **perspective** and focus) as well as at sentence level (the positioning of specific words).

In the beginning of the extract, the writer introduces the character Ojukwu and he becomes centrally important to the plot. Immediately, his unusual name establishes a cultural background to the text, which engages the reader. The quick time-shift through the connective 'by evening' shows the rapid passage of time. At the end of the extract, the discourse marker 'otherwise' foreshadows a dramatic event and builds the reader's expectations towards the cliffhanger on the final line.

Upgrade

Consider why your chosen structural feature is relevant at that specific point in the extract.

Key term

perspective: someone's point of view or attitude towards something

Unit 2: Narrative perspective (Paper 1 Question 3)

Understand it

In Paper 1 Question 3, the phrase 'interest you as a reader' gives you the freedom to include any relevant examples of structure you want. Look at the question below.

Example Exam Question

3 How has the writer structured the text to interest you as a reader?

[8 marks]

What do you understand the word 'interest' to mean in the context of this question? It should remind you to consider the effects of the writer's choices on you as a reader.

Now study the mark scheme for Paper 1 Question 3 again.

Level 4 Perceptive, detailed analysis **7–8 marks**	Shows detailed and perceptive understanding of structural features: • Analyses the effects of the writer's choice of structural features • Selects a judicious range of examples • Makes sophisticated and accurate use of subject terminology
Level 3 Clear, relevant explanation **5–6 marks**	Shows clear understanding of structural features: • Explains clearly the effects of the writer's choice of structural features • Selects a range of relevant examples • Makes clear and accurate use of subject terminology

Activity 1

Paper 1 Question 3 will always tell you to think about the whole of the source. How can you make sure you meet this requirement?

- -

- -

Revise it

Activity 2

a. What different narrative perspectives can writers use?

- -

- -

- -

Learning focus:

- Understand differences in narrative perspective.
- Analyse how the writer's choice of narrative perspective achieves effects.
- Use subject terminology accurately.

Upgrade

A judicious range of structural features is not just a list identifying what can be found in the extract. The mark scheme makes it clear that your response will be rewarded for the quality of analysis of the effects of structure, and your examples and use of subject terminology must support this. So avoid just feature spotting!

Upgrade

You could divide the extract into three sections – beginning, middle and end – then make sure you choose a relevant structural feature as an example from each section.

Activity 2 *continued*

b. What is the difference between these narrative perspectives?

----

c. How is the **point of view** from which a story is told different to the narrative perspective?

Key term

point of view: opinion, a way of thinking about something

Read the extract below carefully twice. It is taken from the novel *Ireland* by Frank Delaney, published in 2004. The novel recounts the history of Ireland as the main character embarks on an epic journey around the country.

Ireland by Frank Delaney

Wonderfully, it was the boy who saw him first. He glanced out of his bedroom window, then looked again and harder – and dared to hope. No, it was not a trick of the light; a tall figure in a ragged black coat and a ruined old hat was walking down the darkening
5   hillside; and he was heading toward the house.

The stranger's face was chalk-white with exhaustion, and he stumbled on the rough ground, his hands held out before him like a sleepwalker's. He looked like a scarecrow deserting his post. High grasses soaked his cracked boots and drenched his coat hems. A
10   mist like a silver veil floated above the ground, broke at his knees, and reassembled itself in his wake. In this twilight fog, mysterious shapes appeared and dematerialized, so that the pale walker was never sure he had seen merely the branches of trees or the arms of mythic dancers come to greet him. Closer in, the dark shadows of
15   the tree trunks twisted into harsh and threatening faces.

Across the fields he saw the yellow glow of lamplight in the window of a house, and he raised his eyes to the sky in some kind of thanks. With no fog on high, the early stars glinted like grains of salt. He became aware of cattle nearby, not yet taken
20   indoors in this mild winter. Many lay curled on the grass where they chewed the cud. As he passed, one or two lurched to their feet in alarm and lumbered off.

And in the house ahead, the boy, nine years old and blond as hay, raced downstairs, calling wildly to his father.

Activity 3

a. Identify the writer's narrative perspective in the extract.

----

b. There are several points of view in the extract. Identify them.

----

c. Explain how you know that there are several points of view.

----

d. What would be the effect of telling the story through a first-person narration by the boy?

Complete the table below by responding to the questions in it.

Where am I?	
Who is here?	
Whose views am I hearing?	
Can I trust their view?	

e. Where does the point of view change from the boy's perspective to the stranger's, and where does it change to an omniscient narrator? Mark these on the extract.

Activity 4

a. The first paragraph gives the boy's perspective whereas the third gives the stranger's perspective. The other paragraphs feature an omniscient narrator. Consider the purpose and effects of the writer's choices and changes of perspective. For each possible explanation below, decide whether you agree or disagree, and justify your choice.

1. | The change in point of view from the boy to the stranger shows that the boy's perspective is not important, so the reader will not expect him to be important in the story.

----

2. | The boy's perspective is significant because he will notice different things about the stranger from an adult observer.

----

3. | The juxtaposition of the boy's and the stranger's perspectives suggests that there may be interaction, conflict or a relationship between these two characters.

----

b. As part of narrative perspective, writers move between external actions and internal thoughts. Read the first and final paragraphs again. Explain why the writer moves between the external actions of the boy and the internal thoughts of the stranger.

Try it with support

The next part of the story tells us that the stranger is a storyteller who is hoping to tell his stories to the boy and his family in exchange for food and lodging. Rejoin the story in the extract below, when the stranger is invited in by the boy's father.

Ireland by Frank Delaney

The man extended a cold, bony hand to the boy peeking around his father's waist.

"A fine boy. God save you too, ma'am!" called the Storyteller to the woman of the house.

5 She looked irked, and he guessed that he, this stringy, unwashed man, with skin like canvas, would disrupt her rigorous household; nonetheless she set a place for him while her husband, pleased and comfortable, poured the visitor a drink.

The boy watched the stranger attacking the food like a tired
10 hound. He sensed that the man's hunger fought with the man's decorum. Nobody spoke because the newcomer seemed too famished to be interrupted. The boy examined the man's face, saw the long, thin scar, wondered if he had been in a knife fight, perhaps with a sailor on some foreign quayside.

15 And the sodden boots – in his mind he saw the stranger fording streams, climbing out of gullies, traversing slopes of limestone shale on his endless travels across the country. Did he have a dog? Seemingly not, which was a pity, since a dog could have sat guard by the fire at night. Did the man ever sleep in caves? They said that
20 bears and wolves had long been extinct in Ireland – but had they?

Activity 5

a. In different colours, highlight the different narrative perspectives of the boy, the stranger and the omniscient narrator.

b. What is the purpose and effect of the writer's choices of perspective? (Look back at your ideas from Activities 3 and 4 as a starting point.) Write one or two paragraphs on a separate piece of paper.

Key term

mood: the feeling or atmosphere created by a piece of writing

Activity 6

a. What details can you see in this later part of the story that link back to the first section?

b. Why do you think the writer has done this? Write your answers on a separate piece of paper.

Activity 7

Read the following example exam question.

Example Exam Question

3 You now need to think about the **whole** of the source.

This text is from the beginning of a novel.

How has the writer structured the text to interest you as a reader?

You could write about:

• what the writer focuses your attention on at the beginning of the source

• how and why the writer changes the focus as the source develops

• any other structural features that interest you.

[8 marks]

a. Use your notes to complete the spider diagram on narrative perspective below to show how the writer of *Ireland* uses narrative structure to interest you as a reader.

b. Now respond in full to the example exam question at the start of this activity. Use a separate piece of paper. You could start like this:

> The writer uses third-person narration but changes the narrative point of view to link the characters of the boy and the storyteller. He begins with...

Remember to consider how the writer uses narrative structure to help the reader engage with a **mood**, theme or character at different points in the story.

41

Unit 3: Analysing the effects of structural features (Paper 1 Question 3)

Understand it

Paper 1 Question 3 asks you to make a detailed analysis of the structural features the writer has chosen. Structural features can be at whole-text level, paragraph level or at sentence level.

Activity 1

Think back to Unit 1 (page 28) where you identified structural devices at whole-text, paragraph and sentence level. Revise your knowledge by identifying a structural feature at each level.

- A structural feature at whole-text level:

- A structural feature at paragraph level:

- A structural feature at sentence level:

Learning focus:
- Analyse the effects of structure.
- Select a range of judicious examples of structural features.
- Interrogate a text.

Upgrade

The best responses will give a detailed analysis of structure by offering an overview of whole-text structure before focusing on specific examples at paragraph and sentence level.

Activity 2

Interrogating a text means asking certain critical questions about it. This will help you to put the text into context and to analyse it.

a. The table below lists critical questions you could ask to interrogate a text. Fill in the appropriate area of focus for each pair of questions from the following options.

interrogate the writer   gaps and silence   time   narrative perspective   characters

Critical questions	Area of focus
Who is in the extract? Why are they introduced at that point?	

Activity 2 continued

Who or what is missing from the extract? What or who has been left out?	
When was the extract written? What is the gender of the writer?	
Does the extract move chronologically? Is there a climactic moment? Where?	
Whose views am I hearing? Can I trust their views?	

b. Now add further questions for each area of focus to support you in interrogating the text.

An extract in an exam paper could contain any of a wide range of structural features, so it is important that you can identify and analyse a wide range too. It is up to you to choose the features that you think are most relevant and that you can analyse in the most detail. That is what being 'judicious' means. The examiner won't award marks for you just knowing the correct subject terminology. To achieve Level 4 in the mark scheme, you have to be able to *analyse the effects* of the writer's choice of structural features'.

Upgrade

Once you know how structure works, you can use it more effectively in your own writing. Try introducing some structural features in the next writing task you complete.

Revise it

Activity 3

a. At whole-text level, you can plot perspective shifts. What is a perspective shift?

----

b. A student achieving the highest marks for Paper 1 Question 3 is able to analyse how a writer moves from inside to outside across a text. This doesn't just mean literal shifts of location, it also means moving from what a character is thinking inside their head to what is happening outside and around them.

Look back at the extracts in Units 1 and 2 of this chapter. Are there any shifts from inside to outside or outside to inside?

- *The Last Days of Ojukwu* (page 30)

- *Ireland* (1) (page 37)

- *Ireland* (2) (page 40)

At paragraph level, a writer creates **cohesion**. This is the 'glue' that links and holds sentences together. Cohesion links new and old information and controls the flow of sentences. It can also act as a signpost to the reader of the direction the text is going to take.

> **Key term**
>
> **cohesion:** the way a piece of writing links together in terms of vocabulary, phrases, clauses, sentences and paragraphs

Activity 4

Match each cohesive device below to its correct purpose by drawing a line between the two.

Cohesive device	Purpose
contrast (e.g. but, whereas, although)	explains why a change occurs
cause and effect (e.g. consequently, since, so)	develops sequence and signals time
qualifying (e.g. although, unless)	explains why something happened
order (e.g. simultaneously, later, ultimately)	signals an opinion
attitude (e.g. fortunately, strangely, surprisingly)	compares

At sentence level, you should consider structural features that contribute to the extract as a whole.

Read the extract below carefully twice. It is taken from the novel *Lipstick Jungle* by Candace Bushnell, published in 2005. This part of the story is set in Manhattan, New York at the end of September. It is New York Fashion Week.

Upgrade

In order to show that short sentences, repetition and patterns are being used as structural devices, you must analyse the position of them in the extracts.

Lipstick Jungle by Candace Bushnell

On Sixth Avenue behind the Public Library, Bryant Park was transformed into a wonderland of white tents where dozens of fashion shows would take place. Black carpeted steps led up to French doors, and all week, these steps were lined with
5 students and fans hoping to get a glimpse of their favorite designers or stars, with Japanese photographers (whom everyone agreed were more polite), with paparazzi, with security men with headsets and walkie-talkies, with the young P.R. girls (always in black, sporting concerned expressions), and with
10 all manner of well-heeled attendees shouting into cell phones for their cars. The curb was lined with black town cars three vehicles deep, as if some terribly important state funeral were about to take place. But inside the tents, life was at its most glamorous and exciting.

15 There were always five or six big shows at which attendance was required to secure one's place in the social pecking order (or to simply remind everyone that you still exist), and the very first of these events was the Victory Ford show, held at seven p.m. on the first Thursday evening of Fashion Week. By six forty-five,
20 the scene inside the tents was one of controlled pandemonium: there were six camera crews, a hundred or so photographers, and a throng of fashionistas, socialites, buyers, and lesser stars, eagerly awaiting the show with the anticipation of an opening night crowd. A young socialite who was cradling a small
25 dachshund in her arms was hit in the back of the head by a video camera; someone else's Jimmy Choo slingback was trod on by one of the P.R. girls who nearly ran her over in order to get to someone more important. Those hoping to get a glimpse of a famous movie star were thwarted, however, because movie
30 stars (and important political people, like the mayor) never went in the front entrance. They were escorted by security to a secret side entrance that led to the backstage area. And in this world, where life is a series of increasingly smaller circles of exclusivity (or Dante's circles of hell, depending on how you look at it),
35 hanging out backstage before the show began was the only place to be.

In the back corner of this area, hidden behind a rack of clothing, stood Victory Ford herself, surreptitiously smoking a cigarette. Victory had quit smoking years ago, but the cigarette was an
40 excuse to have a moment to herself. For three minutes, everyone

would leave her alone, giving her a few seconds to focus and prepare for the next sixty minutes, in which she had to attend to the last-minute details of the show, schmooze with her celebrity clients, and give several interviews to the print and television

45 press. She frowned, taking a drag on the cigarette, wanting to savor this one moment of peace. She'd been working eighteen-hour days in the four weeks before the show, and yet, this next crucial hour would pass in what felt like a second. She dropped the cigarette butt into a half-empty glass of champagne.

50 She looked at her watch – an elegant stainless-steel Baume & Mercier with a row of tiny diamonds along the face – and took a deep breath. <u>It was six-fifty</u>. By eight p.m., when the last model had completed her turn on the runway and Victory went out to take her bow, she would know her fate for the coming year. She would be
55 either on top of the game; in the middle and surviving; or on the bottom, trying to regain her position. She knew she was taking a risk with this show, and she also knew she hadn't had to. Any other designer would have continued along the same lines that had made them so successful for the past three years, but Victory couldn't
60 do that. <u>It was too easy</u>. Tonight, she hoped to show the industry a new side to her talents, a new way to look at how women might dress. She was, she thought wryly, either a hero or a fool.

Activity 5

There are two short sentences in the final paragraph of the extract, which have been underlined for you.

a. Rank the explanations below according to how well they analyse the purpose of the first short sentence (with 1 being the best analysis).

> The short sentence 'It was six-fifty' tells us the time of the show is near, which builds anticipation and allows the reader to feel the nervousness of Victory Ford. The position of this sentence is important because it is in chronological order, so the show is getting closer. The reader is waiting for the show to start and feels that it is important. ☐

> The short sentence 'It was six-fifty' comes immediately after we are told that the character takes a 'deep breath', which suggests she is preparing herself and fighting her nerves before the show. This builds tension and links with the following words, 'By eight p.m.', as time is passing quickly for the character. There are many references to time in the whole extract ('a few seconds', 'next sixty minutes'), which create cohesion across the whole extract and suggests time is a pressure on the character and invading her thoughts. ☐

> The short sentence 'It was six-fifty' tells us that it is ten minutes to seven and the show will be finished by eight o'clock. This tells the reader that the show will be over quickly. It is interesting for the reader to know how long it is until the show starts and how long it will last so they can understand the character's feelings. ☐

Activity 5 *continued*

b. Justify your choices.

----

c. Write a full explanation of the effects of the writer's use of the other short sentence in this paragraph, 'It was too easy.'

Upgrade

Remember to consider the position of the sentence and make reference to the text as a whole.

Try it with support

Activity 6

a. Each paragraph in the extract has a different topic. Write the appropriate paragraph number against each topic below.

- Victory Ford's thoughts
- Description of the location of the Victory Ford show
- Description of the location of Fashion Week
- Introduction to the character of Victory Ford

Activity 6 *continued*

b. On the extract, label where the writer shifts the location from outside to inside. What is the effect of this?

----

c. On the extract, label where the writer shifts the perspective from outside to inside the character's head. What is the effect of this?

Activity 7

a. Label the structural features in the extract that you know you can analyse successfully.

b. Pick the four features you could analyse in the most detail and rank them in the order you would analyse them. Make sure you include a new structural feature you have learned about in this unit.

----

c. Using the four features you have selected, write a full analysis of how the writer of *Lipstick Jungle* uses structure to interest the reader.

Upgrade

When you make your choice, try to cover the whole text and select a range of features. Consider whole-text level, paragraph level and sentence level.

Now look at another example exam question.

3 You now need to think about the **whole** of the source.

This text is from the middle of a novel.

How has the writer structured the text to interest you as a reader?

You could write about:

• what the writer focuses your attention on at the beginning of the source

• how and why the writer changes this focus as the source develops

• any other structural features that interest you.

[8 marks]

This extract is from the novel *A Room With a View* by E.M. Forster, published in 1908. The character Cecil has just asked Mrs Honeychurch for permission to marry her daughter Lucy. He is now in the garden with Lucy while Mrs Honeychurch is indoors writing a letter.

A Room With a View by E.M. Forster

"Will this do?" called his mother. "'Dear Mrs. Vyse, – Cecil has just asked my permission about it, and I should be delighted if Lucy wishes it.' Then I put in at the top, 'and I have told Lucy so.' I must write the letter out again – 'and I have told Lucy so. But Lucy seems very

5 uncertain, and in these days young people must decide for themselves.' I said that because I didn't want Mrs. Vyse to think us old-fashioned. She goes in for lectures and improving her mind, and all the time a thick layer of **flue** under the beds, and the maid's dirty thumb-marks where you turn on the electric light. She keeps that flat abominably –"

10 "Suppose Lucy marries Cecil, would she live in a flat, or in the country?"

"Don't interrupt so foolishly. Where was I? Oh yes – 'Young people must decide for themselves. I know that Lucy likes your son, because she tells me everything, and she wrote to me from Rome when he asked her first.' No, I'll cross that last bit out – it looks patronizing. I'll stop at

15 'because she tells me everything.' Or shall I cross that out, too?"

"Cross it out, too," said Freddy.

Mrs. Honeychurch left it in.

"Then the whole thing runs: 'Dear Mrs. Vyse. – Cecil has just asked my permission about it, and I should be delighted if Lucy wishes it, and I

20 have told Lucy so. But Lucy seems very uncertain, and in these days young people must decide for themselves. I know that Lucy likes your son, because she tells me everything. But I do not know – "

"Look out!" cried Freddy.

The curtains parted.

25 Cecil's first movement was one of irritation. He couldn't bear the Honeychurch habit of sitting in the dark to save the furniture. Instinctively he gave the curtains a twitch, and sent them swinging down their poles. Light entered. There was revealed a terrace, such as is owned by many villas with trees each side of it, and on it a little rustic seat, and two

30 flower-beds. But it was transfigured by the view beyond, for Windy Corner was built on the range that overlooks the **Sussex Weald**. Lucy, who was in the little seat, seemed on the edge of a green magic carpet which hovered in the air above the tremulous world.

Cecil entered.

35 Appearing thus late in the story, Cecil must be at once described. He was medieval. Like a Gothic statue. Tall and refined, with shoulders that seemed braced square by an effort of the will, and a head that was tilted a little higher than the usual level of vision, he resembled those **fastidious** saints who guard the portals of a French cathedral. Well educated, well

40 endowed, and not deficient physically, he remained in the grip of a certain devil whom the modern world knows as self-consciousness, and whom the medieval, with dimmer vision, worshipped as **asceticism**. A Gothic statue implies celibacy, just as a Greek statue implies fruition [...].

Mrs. Honeychurch left her letter on the writing table and moved towards

45 her young acquaintance.

"Oh, Cecil!" she exclaimed – "oh, Cecil, do tell me!"

"I promessi sposi," said he.

They stared at him anxiously.

"She has accepted me," he said, and the sound of the thing in English

50 made him flush and smile with pleasure, and look more human.

Glossary

flue: dirt from the chimney

Sussex Weald: an area in south-east England known for its rural beauty

fastidious: fussy and attentive to detail

asceticism: strong self-discipline, often for religious reasons

Activity 8

Using the method you have practised in this chapter, write your response to the question on a separate sheet of paper.

Progress check

	I'm confident	I need more practice	I'm not confident
I can identify the focus at different points in a text and why the writer made this choice.			
I can identify how a text is sequenced, why the writer chose to do that and how the sequence relates to the intended meaning.			
I can identify how I am left feeling at the end of a text and how/why the writer chose to do that.			
I can identify and select a range of judicious examples of structural features.			
I can analyse in detail the following structural features:			
• cohesive devices			
• flashback			
• perspective shift			
• chronological order			
• pattern/sequence			
• discourse marker			
• omniscient narrator			
• introductions			
• conclusions			
I can use subject terminology in a relevant, accurate and sophisticated way.			

Unit 1: Using comprehension skills (Paper 1 Question 4)

Understand it

Paper 1 Question 4 is an evaluation question. You will be asked to **critically evaluate** a statement based on a source text. This means that you are expected to show your understanding of what the writer says and analyse how they use language and structure to say it.

Comprehension skills + analysis skills = critical evaluation

Activity 1

Take a look at how Question 4 will be phrased, then complete the activities that follow.

Example Exam Question

> **4** Focus this part of your answer on the second part of the source, from **line xx to the end**.
>
> A reader said, 'Alice seems to regret her actions. She seems anxious about what other people may think of her.'
>
> To what extent do you agree?
>
> In your response, you could:
>
> • consider your own impressions of Alice and her actions
>
> • evaluate how the writer conveys Alice's anxiety
>
> • support your response with references to the text.
>
> **[20 marks]**

a. Identify the main focus of the student's statement.

----

b. You will note that the statement is followed by 'to what extent do you agree'. What does this suggest you have to do?

----

c. Which of the bullet points is clearly asking you to write about Alice and which is asking you to write about what the writer is doing?

Learning focus:

• Understand the mark scheme and examiner expectations for Paper 1 Question 4.

• Make a convincing and critical response to the focus of Question 4.

• Select judicious quotations to support the response.

• Make perceptive inferences based on the text.

Upgrade

You should spend 25 minutes answering Paper 1 Question 4. It is worth 20 marks and makes up 25% of the entire paper.

Key terms

critical evaluation: weighing up and giving an interpretation of the text using your comprehension skills *and* your analytical skills

writer's methods: ways of using linguistic and structural features

Take a look at the mark scheme below. Remember that '**writer's methods**' means ways of using linguistic features *and* structural features. Also note the importance of supporting your answer with close reference to the text.

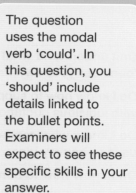

Upgrade

The question uses the modal verb 'could'. In this question, you 'should' include details linked to the bullet points. Examiners will expect to see these specific skills in your answer.

Level 4 Perceptive, detailed, evaluation 16–20 marks	Shows perceptive and detailed evaluation: • Evaluates critically and in detail the effect(s) on the reader • Shows perceptive understanding of writer's methods • Selects a range of judicious textual detail • Develops a convincing and critical response to the focus of the statement
Level 3 Clear, relevant evaluation 11–15 marks	Shows clear and relevant evaluation: • Evaluates clearly the effect(s) on the reader • Shows clear understanding of writer's methods • Selects a range of relevant textual references • Makes a clear and relevant response to the focus of the statement

Activity 2

Look at the bullet points from the example exam question. Which of the highlighted sections in the mark scheme match each bullet point? Circle the correct answer.

a. 'consider your own impressions of Alice and her actions'   green / yellow

b. 'evaluate how the writer conveys Alice's anxiety'   green / yellow

Activity 3

Look at these important terms from the mark scheme. Draw lines to match them up with the correct definition.

Term	Definition
judicious	noticing and understanding things that not many people notice; picking up on subtle details
convincing	giving a finely judged opinion
critical	well chosen or with good judgement
developed	believable and persuasive
evaluate	detailed and powerful
perceptive	to weigh up or judge something

Lots of these definitions are about making judgements. Paper 1 Question 4 is where your understanding and analytical skill is measured through your ability to weigh up and interpret a text by considering:

• what the writer is saying

• how they are saying it.

Before you start looking at this question in more detail, it is important to be honest with yourself and ask:

	I'm confident	I need more practice	I'm not confident
Do I understand what it means to 'consider your own impressions'?			
Do I know how to support answers with judicious quotations from the text?			
Do I know what methods a writer uses to convey ideas or feelings?			
Do I know how to comment on the effects of methods to show that I have a perceptive understanding?			

Revise it

For Question 4 you will not be working on a printed extract from the source as for Question 2, nor will you be working with the whole source as for Question 3. Instead, you will be asked to work from a short section of the source, of approximately 15 lines long. The section may well contain the ending of the text, a twist or a turning point in the narrative.

Read the extract opposite, which is taken from the novel *A Thousand Splendid Suns* by Khaled Hosseini, published in 2007. It is set in Afghanistan. In it, a teenage girl, Mariam, has had an arranged marriage to Rasheed, a shoemaker thirty years older than her. She has moved away from home to live in the capital city, Kabul, with her new husband.

Look at the following example exam question.

Example Exam Question

4 A reader said, 'This part of the story, where Mariam now lives with her husband Rasheed, suggests that she is desperately unhappy.'

To what extent do you agree?

In your response, you could:

- consider the reasons why Mariam is unhappy
- evaluate how the writer creates a sense of Mariam's unhappiness
- support your response with references to the text.

[20 marks]

In order to answer this question effectively, you should spend 10 minutes planning and organising your response. Your first five minutes of planning time should focus on the first and third bullet points of the task:

- consider the reasons why Mariam is unhappy
- support your response with references to the text.

These call upon your comprehension skills and address the 'what' element of the task.

A Thousand Splendid Suns by Khaled Hosseini

The first few days, Mariam hardly left her room. She was awakened every dawn for prayer by the distant cry of **azan**, after which she crawled back into bed. She was still in bed when she heard Rasheed in the bathroom, washing up, when he came into
5   her room to check on her before he went to his shop. From her window, she watched him in the yard, securing his lunch in the rear carrier pack of his bicycle, then walking his bicycle across the yard and into the street. She watched him pedal away, saw his broad, thick-shouldered figure disappear around the turn at
10   the end of the street. For most of the days, Mariam stayed in bed, feeling adrift and forlorn. Sometimes she went downstairs to the kitchen, ran her hands over the sticky, greasy-stained counter; the vinyl, flowered curtains that smelled like burned meals. She looked through the ill-fitting drawers at the mismatched spoons
15   and knives, the colander and chipped, wooden spatulas, these would-be instruments of her new daily life, all reminding her of the havoc that had struck her life, making her feel uprooted, displaced, like an intruder on someone else's life.

Glossary

azan: the Islamic call to prayer broadcast from a mosque

Activity 4

a. Look closely at the question and highlight the focus of the student's statement. What is your initial response to it? Jot down your first feelings and ideas below.

----

b. Now re-read the extract. You need to select no more than three judicious quotations that would support your response and illustrate the 'what'. These questions may help:

- What are the reasons for Mariam's unhappiness?

- What do we learn about her that suggests she is unhappy?

- What do we understand from the extract about her unhappiness?

Highlight your chosen quotations on the extract. An example has been done to get you started.

Activity 4 *continued*

c. Now look closely at your selected quotations. Annotate each one. What does each quotation:

- imply about Mariam?

- suggest to you about her unhappiness?

- tell you about her life and feelings at this point in the story?

Try it with support

The annotations you have made on the extract are your **inferences**.

Using Statement, Quotation, Inference (SQI) to approach the 'what' element of the question will help you to organise your response.

You should:

- make a strong statement that links directly with the focus of the statement

- support this statement with a well-chosen quotation

- show your understanding by making subtle and finely judged inferences.

> **Key term**
>
> **inferences:** sensible conclusions of what is meant by an author, based on clues given in the text

Activity 5

a. Read the student responses below. Using different coloured pens or highlighters, in each example identify where you can see the:

- statement
- quotation(s)
- inference(s).

Student A

I agree entirely that Mariam seems desperately unhappy. We see this when we learn that Mariam 'hardly left her room'. This, I feel, suggests she is frightened and withdrawn.

Student B

Mariam's unhappiness is at first suggested to us when we learn that within the 'first few days' of her marriage she 'hardly left her room'. This suggests how Mariam has isolated herself and wishes to remain hidden and separated from her husband. It suggests she does not feel happy or comfortable to be in his presence. It further implies that she is in unfamiliar surroundings and is feeling insecure.

b. Which answer shows Level 3 qualities and which shows Level 4 qualities? What extra skill can you see in the Level 4 response?

Activity 5 *continued*

c. Using the notes and annotations you made on the extract for Activity 4, finish writing Student B's response using the Statement, Quotation, Inference approach and your selected quotations. Remember that at this stage you are thinking about the first and third bullets in the question.

Example Exam Question

4 A reader said, 'This part of the story, where Mariam now lives with her husband Rasheed, suggests she is desperately unhappy.'

To what extent do you agree?

In your response, you could:

- consider the reasons why Mariam is unhappy
- evaluate how the writer creates a sense of Mariam's unhappiness
- support your response with references to the text.

[20 marks]

Unit 2: Analysing the writer's methods and their effects (Paper 1 Question 4)

Understand it

In order to answer Paper 1 Question 4 fully and hit all aspects of the mark scheme, you need to consider and plan for the second and third bullet points of the task.

Example Exam Question

4 A reader said, 'This part of the story, where Mariam now lives with her husband Rasheed, suggests she is desperately unhappy.'

To what extent do you agree?

In your response, you could:

- consider the reasons why Mariam is unhappy
- evaluate how the writer creates a sense of Mariam's unhappiness
- support your response with references to the text.

[20 marks]

These bullet points call upon your analytical skills and address the 'how' element of the task. Remember:

Comprehension skills + analysis skills = critical evaluation

Remind yourself of the mark scheme and the focus of this unit.

Level 4 Perceptive, detailed evaluation **16–20 marks**	Shows perceptive and detailed evaluation: • Evaluates critically and in detail the effect(s) on the reader • Shows perceptive understanding of writer's methods • Selects a range of judicious textual detail • Develops a convincing and critical response to the focus of the statement
Level 3 Clear, relevant evaluation **11–15 marks**	Shows clear and relevant evaluation: • Evaluates clearly the effect(s) on the reader • Shows clear understanding of writer's methods • Selects a range of relevant textual references • Makes a clear and relevant response to the focus of the statement

The phrase 'writer's methods' means any of the features and techniques a writer uses to craft a text. These include all the language features and techniques you thought about in Chapter 2 and all the structural features and techniques you thought about in Chapter 3.

Activity 1

List all the features and techniques you can remember from Chapters 1 and 2 in the table below. Add any others that you know.

Language features and techniques	Structural features and techniques

By evaluating the effects (the second bullet point of the question) you are considering the impact that a writer's chosen method has on you as a reader. This is an even stronger way of measuring your understanding of a text. It is where you can show how deeply you have engaged with the text by expressing the thoughts and feelings the writer has evoked in you through the way they crafted their work.

One way to quickly identify your thoughts on the effect of a writer's method is to ask yourself these questions:

- What is this language feature making me think of or feel or imagine when I read it?

- What is this structural feature doing to or adding to, creating within or shifting within the text?

Revise it

Activity 2

Look again at the extract from *A Thousand Splendid Suns* below. Some of the interesting methods the writer has used to craft this text have been highlighted for you.

Annotate each highlighted section with the language and structural features and techniques the writer is using.

A Thousand Splendid Suns by Khaled Hosseini

The first few days, Mariam hardly left her room. She was awakened every dawn for prayer by the distant cry of azan, after which she crawled back into bed. She was still in bed when she heard Rasheed in the bathroom, washing up, when he came into
5   her room to check on her before he went to his shop. From her window, she watched him in the yard, securing his lunch in the rear carrier pack of his bicycle, then walking his bicycle across the yard and into the street. She watched him pedal away, saw his broad, thick-shouldered figure disappear around the turn at
10   the end of the street. For most of the days, Mariam stayed in bed, feeling adrift and forlorn. Sometimes she went downstairs to the kitchen, ran her hands over the sticky, greasy-stained counter; the vinyl, flowered curtains that smelled like burned meals. She looked through the ill-fitting drawers at the mismatched spoons
15   and knives, the colander and chipped, wooden spatulas, these would-be instruments of her new daily life, all reminding her of the havoc that had struck her life, making her feel uprooted, displaced, like an intruder on someone else's life.

Activity 3

Look back at the features you identified in Activity 2 and annotate the extract further by considering the following questions. These ideas will help you to shape your comments on effect.

a. What kind of sentence opens the extract? What does its bluntness make you feel about Mariam and the situation she is in?

b. What type of phrase is 'crawled back'? What sort of movement does this suggest? What does this make you imagine about Mariam's state of mind at this time?

c. How might the reader react to the phrase 'to check on her'? What possible interpretations might the writer want the reader to consider here?

d. What kind of a phrase is 'broad, thick-shouldered figure'? Why does the writer describe Mariam's new husband like this? What does this make you imagine?

e. Mariam is feeling 'adrift' and 'forlorn'. What kind of words are these? In what context would you normally see the word 'adrift'? What emotions do these words arouse in you?

f. The writer uses two separate techniques to describe the kitchen. Why does he switch to describing this room in the house at this point and what does that description add to the atmosphere?

g. Why might the **adjectives** 'ill-fitting' and 'mismatched' have been chosen? Do they represent something more than the drawers and the spoons themselves? What do you think?

h. What do you think of when you see the word 'havoc'? Does this link with the idea of a newly married couple beginning their life together?

i. What situation might we usually associate with the words 'uprooted' and 'displaced'? What do they convey to us about Mariam's situation? What type of action is suggested?

j. By comparing herself to 'an intruder' what do we imagine about the situation Mariam has found herself in?

Key term

adjective: a word that describes something named by a noun or pronoun

Activity 4

Select two of the features you annotated and feel most confident about.

On a separate piece of paper, write one paragraph about each feature. In each paragraph you should:

- clearly identify the language or structural feature by using the correct terminology

- give precise examples of that feature

- write up your comment on effect from your notes, considering what the feature makes you think, feel or imagine.

61

To build your response, you need to add your work on methods and effects to the work you did on inferential reading in Unit 1 (pages 52–57) to create a critical evaluation:

Comprehension skills + analysis skills = critical evaluation

Look at how the sample student response to the example exam question has now been developed to show analytical skills.

Example Exam Question

4 A reader said, 'This part of the story, where Mariam now lives with her husband Rasheed, suggests she is desperately unhappy.'

To what extent do you agree?

In your response, you could:

- consider the reasons why Mariam is unhappy
- evaluate how the writer creates a sense of Mariam's unhappiness
- support your response with references to the text.

[20 marks]

Mariam's unhappiness is at first suggested to us when we learn that within the 'first few days' of her marriage she 'hardly left her room'. This suggests how Mariam has isolated herself and wishes to remain hidden and separated from her husband. It suggests she does not feel happy or comfortable to be in his presence. It further implies that she is in unfamiliar surroundings and is feeling insecure.

The bluntness of the opening statement makes me feel that Mariam is cut off from the outside world – almost a prisoner – and has no freedom in this new location. The use of the pronoun 'her' is interesting in referring to the room. This creates the effect of an immediate distance in this newly married couple. There is no reference to 'their' room and we are given the impression that Mariam wishes to remain physically separated from her new husband.

Activity 5

On the student response opposite, highlight and label each of the skills listed on the mark scheme on page 58. You could use the annotations below.

- A response to the focus of the statement, with a convincing inference

- A carefully selected quotation from the extract to support the response

- Identification and examples of a method(s) the writer uses to engage the reader

- A thoughtful comment on the effect of this method on the reader

Activity 6

Now that you have looked at the beginning of a sample student response you are going to build a complete response to the same example exam question. Write two more paragraphs of your own that address the bullet points from the task:

- consider the reasons why Mariam is unhappy

- evaluate how the writer creates a sense of Mariam's unhappiness

- support your response with references to the text.

Upgrade

Use your comprehension (Statement, Quotation, Inference) work from Unit 1 on pages 56–57. Add your work on methods from your notes in this unit.

Unit 3: Planning and writing a complete critical evaluation (Paper 1 Question 4)

Understand it

You have now worked on a method that allows you to plan for Paper 1 Question 4 by using both your comprehension and analytical skills. You have also established the key difference between making inferences and commenting on the effects of a writer's choice.

Learning focus:
- Plan a critical evaluation response to show all the required skills.
- Write a response that hits the higher levels of the mark scheme.

Activity 1

In the exam, Paper 1 will take you on a 'journey' through the source text, as shown in the bullet points below.

In your own words, recap what Question 4 will ask you to focus on and what skills you will need to show. If you are unsure, check the information in Units 1 and 2 of this chapter.

- Question 1 will ask you to complete a simple listing exercise based on the first few lines of the source.

- Question 2 will ask you to look at a key paragraph and analyse the choices of vocabulary, language features and techniques, and sentence forms within it.

- Question 3 will ask you to look at the whole text and analyse some of the structural choices made by the writer.

- Question 4 _____

  _____

  _____

  _____

Upgrade

Remember Paper 1 Question 4 is worth 20 marks out of a possible 40 marks for the Reading section. Leave about 5 minutes to plan and 25 minutes to write this response.

Upgrade

By completing Questions 1, 2 and 3 in order you will come to understand the source text and will have examined in detail some of the key methods the writer used to craft it. This is invaluable preparation for Question 4.

Revise it

Activity 2

The source text opposite is taken from the middle of the novel *The Secret History* by Donna Tartt, published in 1992. In it, a group of Classics students from an American university are planning to commit a murder.

Read the extract twice and annotate it with any ideas you have about the mood, the feelings or the atmosphere. Your notes will help you to formulate your interpretation later.

The Secret History by Donna Tartt

It was getting darker by the minute and cold, too. I buttoned up my jacket and sat on a damp rock that overlooked the ravine, staring at the muddy, leaf-clogged rill that trickled below and half listening to the twins argue about what they were going to make for dinner.

5   Francis leaned against a tree, smoking. After a while he put out the cigarette on the sole of his shoe and came over to sit by me.

Minutes passed. The sky was so overcast it was almost purple. A wind swayed through a luminous clump of bushes on the opposite bank, and I shivered. The twins were arguing

10   monotonously. When they were in moods like this – disturbed, upset – they tended to sound like **Heckle and Jeckle**.

All of a sudden Henry emerged from the woods in a flurry of underbrush, wiping his dirt-caked hands on his trousers. "Somebody's coming," he said quietly.

15   The twins stopped talking and blinked at him.

"What?" said Charles.

"Around the back way. Listen."

We were quiet, looking at each other. A chilly breeze rustled through the woods and a gust of white dogwood petals blew into

20   the clearing.

"I don't hear anything," Francis said.

Henry put a finger to his lips. The five of us stood poised, waiting, for a moment longer. I took a breath and was about to speak when all of a sudden I did hear something.

25   Footsteps, the crackle of branches. We looked at one another. Henry bit his lip and glanced around. The ravine was bare, no place to hide, no way for the rest of us to run across the clearing and into the woods without making a lot of noise. He was about to say something when all of a sudden there was a crash of

30   bushes, very near, and he stepped out of the clearing between two trees, like someone ducking into a doorway on a city street.

The rest of us, stranded in the open, looked at each other and then at Henry – thirty feet away, safe at the shady margin of the wood. He waved at us impatiently. I heard the sudden crunch of

35   footsteps on gravel and, hardly aware of what I was doing, turned away spasmodically and pretended to inspect the trunk of a nearby tree.

The footsteps approached. Prickles rising on the nape of my neck, I bent to scrutinize the tree trunk more closely; silvery bark,

40   cool to the touch, ants marching out of a fissure in a glittering black thread.

Then – almost before I noticed it – the footsteps stopped, very near my back.

I glanced up and saw Charles. He was staring straight ahead with

45   a ghastly expression on his face and I was on the verge of asking

him what the matter was when, with a sick, incredulous rush of disbelief, I heard Bunny's voice directly behind me.

"Well, I'll be damned," he said briskly. "What's this? Meeting of the Nature Club?"

50   I turned. It was Bunny, all right, all six-foot-three of him, looming up behind me in a tremendous yellow rain slicker that came almost to his ankles.

There was an awful silence.

Glossary

Heckle and Jeckle: American cartoon characters, twin crows that look for trouble wherever they go

Activity 3

You are now going to plan a response to the following example question.

Example Exam Question

4 Focus this part of your answer on the second part of the source, from **line 10 to the end**.

A reader said, 'This part of the story creates a real atmosphere of tension and suspense.'

To what extent do you agree?

In your response, you could:

- consider what is happening to create the atmosphere
- evaluate how the writer creates an atmosphere of **tension** and suspense
- support your response with references to the text.

[20 marks]

a. Begin planning for this task by selecting three key areas of the extract that directly link to the first bullet point. Exactly what is happening in the extract to create the atmosphere? Select three quotations that demonstrate this.

b. Now annotate each of your chosen quotations with the inferences you can draw from them. What does each quotation suggest to you about the atmosphere? What is implied that creates tension and suspense?

Upgrade

At this planning stage, when you are gathering ideas, your quotations could be quite lengthy. When you write up your ideas, you can pinpoint more judiciously the precise phrases you need to support each statement.

Key term

tension: the feeling of waiting, as though something is about to happen

Now you need to **deconstruct** your quotations, taking them apart and looking at the separate key elements. You have a choice of focusing in on a key language feature or of discussing a structural choice the writer has made. Aim to work on three key features.

Commenting on language features

You could choose to comment on the effects of language features in your response.

Activity 4

a. Copy out two of your selected quotations below. Underline an interesting aspect of vocabulary or a language feature in each quotation.

b. Then analyse each chosen feature with a comment on its effect. Ask yourself: what is this language feature making me think of, feel or imagine when I read it?

For example:

noun phrases

'He was staring straight ahead with <u>a ghastly expression</u> on his face and I was on the verge of asking him what the matter was when, with <u>a sick, incredulous rush</u> of disbelief, I heard Bunny's voice directly behind me.'

Effect: The noun phrases make me think that the character Charles is horrified or experiencing a great fear. I feel that the narrator's response is a physical response to the fear in the air, suggesting he experiences nausea. The word 'rush' implies an alarming suddenness. It makes me feel that the arrival of Bunny is either unwelcome or unexpected.

1. _____

_____

_____

Effect: _____

_____

_____

_____

2. _____

_____

_____

Effect: _____

_____

_____

_____

Commenting on structural features

Alternatively, you could choose to comment on the effects of structural features.

Activity 5

a. Copy out two of your selected quotations below. Underline an interesting structural feature in each quotation.

b. Then analyse each chosen feature with a comment on its effect. Ask yourself: what is this structural feature doing to or adding to, creating within or shifting within the text?

For example:

| foregrounding | 'Footsteps, the crackle of branches.' | minor sentence |

The minor sentence brings the reader up short and creates a dramatic, sharp pause. It is more effective because there is no subject or verb in the minor sentence so the writer uses this to prevent the reader (and the narrator) from knowing who is coming. The word 'Footsteps' is foregrounded in the minor sentence. This positioning puts emphasis on the sound of approaching danger (reinforced by the onomatopoeic 'crackle') and also masks the identity of whoever is approaching, adding to the mystery and suspense.

1. _____

_____

_____

Effect: _____

_____

_____

_____

2. _____

_____

_____

Effect: _____

_____

_____

_____

Activity 6

a. Piece together all your notes and ideas in a complete response to the question on *The Secret History*. Write on a separate piece of paper. Aim to write three paragraphs. To hit all aspects of the Level 4 mark scheme, in each paragraph you should:

- make a precise and definite statement in response to the focus

- use well-chosen quotations to support your points

- show your understanding by making a thoughtful, perceptive inference

- zoom in to identify a language or structural feature

- give an example of it precisely and judiciously

- comment on the effect of the feature in detail, developing your ideas.

b. Annotate your response to show where you have shown these skills.

Example Exam Question

4 Focus this part of your answer on the second part of the source, from **line 10 to the end**.

A reader said, 'This part of the story creates a real atmosphere of tension and suspense.'

To what extent do you agree?

In your response, you could:

- consider what is happening to create the atmosphere

- evaluate how the writer creates an atmosphere of tension and suspense

- support your response with references to the text.

[20 marks]

Try it with support

Read the source and then the example exam question below. The source is from *A Room With a View* by E.M. Forster. (You used it on pages 49–50 to practise Paper 1 Question 3.) In it, the character of Cecil has asked Mrs Honeychurch for permission to marry her daughter Lucy.

A Room With a View by E.M. Forster (1908)

"Will this do?" called his mother. "'Dear Mrs. Vyse, – Cecil has just asked my permission about it, and I should be delighted if Lucy wishes it.' Then I put in at the top, 'and I have told Lucy so.' I must write the letter out again – 'and I have told Lucy so. But Lucy seems very uncertain, and in these days young people must decide for themselves.' I said that
5   because I didn't want Mrs. Vyse to think us old-fashioned. She goes in for lectures and improving her mind, and all the time a thick layer of **flue** under the beds, and the maid's dirty thumb-marks where you turn on the electric light. She keeps that flat abominably –"

"Suppose Lucy marries Cecil, would she live in a flat, or in the country?"

10 "Don't interrupt so foolishly. Where was I? Oh yes – 'Young people must decide for themselves. I know that Lucy likes your son, because she tells me everything, and she wrote to me from Rome when he asked her first.' No, I'll cross that last bit out – it looks patronizing. I'll stop at 'because she tells me everything.' Or shall I cross that out, too?"

"Cross it out, too," said Freddy.

Mrs. Honeychurch left it in.

15 "Then the whole thing runs: 'Dear Mrs. Vyse. – Cecil has just asked my permission about it, and I should be delighted if Lucy wishes it, and I have told Lucy so. But Lucy seems very uncertain, and in these days young people must decide for themselves. I know that Lucy likes your son, because she tells me everything. But I do not know –'"

"Look out!" cried Freddy.

20 The curtains parted.

Cecil's first movement was one of irritation. He couldn't bear the Honeychurch habit of sitting in the dark to save the furniture. Instinctively he gave the curtains a twitch, and sent them swinging down their poles. Light entered. There was revealed a terrace, such as is owned by many villas with trees each side of it, and on it a little rustic seat, and two
25 flower-beds. But it was transfigured by the view beyond, for Windy Corner was built on the range that overlooks the **Sussex Weald**. Lucy, who was in the little seat, seemed on the edge of a green magic carpet which hovered in the air above the tremulous world.

Cecil entered.

Appearing thus late in the story, Cecil must be at once described. He was medieval.
30 Like a Gothic statue. Tall and refined, with shoulders that seemed braced square by an effort of the will, and a head that was tilted a little higher than the usual level of vision, he resembled those **fastidious** saints who guard the portals of a French cathedral. Well educated, well endowed, and not deficient physically, he remained in the grip of a certain devil whom the modern world knows as self-consciousness, and
35 whom the medieval, with dimmer vision, worshipped as **asceticism**. A Gothic statue implies celibacy, just as a Greek statue implies fruition [...].

Mrs. Honeychurch left her letter on the writing table and moved towards her young acquaintance.

"Oh, Cecil!" she exclaimed – "oh, Cecil, do tell me!"

40 "I promessi sposi," said he.

They stared at him anxiously.

"She has accepted me," he said, and the sound of the thing in English made him flush and smile with pleasure, and look more human.

Glossary

flue: dirt from the chimney
Sussex Weald: an area in south-east England known for its rural beauty

fastidious: fussy and attentive to detail
asceticism: strong self-discipline, often for religious reasons

Example Exam Question

4   Focus this part of your answer on the second part of the source, from **line 20 to the end**.

A reader said, 'This part of the story, where Cecil comes into the room, tells us a great deal about his attitudes and personality.'

To what extent do you agree?

In your response, you could:

- consider what we learn about Cecil's attitudes and personality

- evaluate how the writer shows Cecil's attitudes and personality

- support your response with references to the text.

[20 marks]

Activity 7

a. Plan your response by selecting your material and annotating the extract with your thoughts and ideas to show your comprehension skills and your analytical skills.

b. Write up your response on a separate sheet of paper. You should aim to write three paragraphs. To hit all aspects of the Level 4 mark scheme, in each paragraph you should:

- make a precise and definite statement in response to the focus

- use well-chosen quotations to support your points

- show your understanding by making a thoughtful, perceptive inference

- zoom in to identify a language or structural feature

- give an example of it precisely and judiciously

- comment on the effect of the feature in detail, developing your ideas.

Progress check

	I'm confident	I need more practice	I'm not confident
I understand what the evaluation question is asking for.			
I know how to support answers with judicious quotations from the text.			
I can identify the methods a writer uses to convey ideas and feelings.			
I can comment on the effects of the writer's methods to show that I have a perceptive understanding.			

Unit 1: Using comprehension skills (Paper 2 Question 4)

Understand it

Paper 2 Question 4 is a comparison question. It is worth 16 marks and is the highest mark for a reading question on Paper 2. It tests a range of the skills you will already have used in other questions on the paper. You need to show perceptive inference (as you do in Question 2) and language or structural analysis (Question 3).

The key element of this question is the ability to apply these skills across two texts, comparing the writers' points of view on a given topic.

Activity 1

Look at the way Paper 2 Question 4 is laid out. Which bullet point refers to the 'what' (AO1) and which to the 'how' (AO2)?

> **Example Exam Question**
>
> **4** For this question, you need to refer to the **whole of Source A**, together with the **whole of Source B**.
>
> Compare how the writers convey their different views and **perspectives** on transport.
>
> In your answer, you could:
>
> - compare their different views and perspectives
> - compare the methods the writers use to convey their different views and perspectives
> - support your response with references to both texts.
>
> **[16 marks]**

Activity 2

The elements of the question also match the ladder of skills in the mark scheme.

a. Using your knowledge of the mark scheme, fill in the gaps in the table opposite.

Upgrade

You should spend around 20 minutes on Paper 2 Question 4 (this does not include your reading time). You should spend about around 5–7 minutes on planning and the rest of the time on writing.

Upgrade

As with Paper 1 Question 4, this Question 4 uses the word 'could'. Really, you 'should' include details linked to the bullet points.

Activity 2 *continued*

b. What is the main difference between the first and fourth bullet points in the mark scheme?

Example Exam Question

4 Compare how the writers convey their different views and perspectives on transport.

In your answer, you could:

- compare their different views and perspectives

- compare the methods the writers use to convey their different views and perspectives

- support your response with references to both texts.

Level _____ P_____, d_____ comparison **13–16 marks**	• Compares ideas and perspectives in a perceptive way • Analyses how writers' methods are used • Selects a range of judicious supporting detail from both texts • Shows a detailed understanding of the different ideas and perspectives in both texts
Level 3 C_____, r_____ comparison **9–12 marks**	• Compares ideas and perspectives in a clear and relevant way • Explains clearly how writers' methods are used • Selects relevant textual detail to support from both texts • Shows a clear understanding of the different ideas and perspectives in both texts

Upgrade

The key point about Paper 2 Question 4 is that it is focusing on the writers and what their thoughts/feelings/perspectives and **point of view** are. It is not just about the content of the texts. You need to be 'inside' the text looking out!

Interpreting writers' perspectives

You will need to compare the writers' ideas and perspectives on a specific focus. In order to do this effectively and perceptively, you must make sure you can interpret:

- their feelings

- what they think

- their overall position and point of view.

Activity 3

a. Look at the sentences below. What is the perspective of each writer? Use the bullet points on page 73 to help you get inside each writer's point of view.

b. Highlight the words that inform you of each perspective.

1. War is never the solution. It causes more problems than it solves and there are always innocent casualties.

- -

2. War is the ultimate show of commitment. We should all be willing to fight for what we believe in.

- -

3. War is a necessary evil. Weapons manufacturing is a huge industry that pumps billions into the economy. Without war less money would be spent.

- -

So, the recipe for success at Grade 6–9 is to:

- compare the ideas and perspectives of the writers in a thoughtful and thorough way
- cover more than one idea or point of view. This enables you to analyse layers of meaning
- select a range of words or features of language and/or structure, using accurate subject terminology
- write a developed analysis on the effects of these examples
- demonstrate accurate and deep understanding in order to be 'perceptive' for Level 4.

Before you start revising for this task, it's important to check your understanding of what the question demands:

	I'm confident	I need more practice	I'm not confident
Do I understand the importance of comparing the texts?			
Do I understand what is meant by ideas and perspective?			
Do I understand how the question is made up of 'what' and 'how'?			

Revise it

For Question 4 you will be working with whole texts. You will need to practice skimming and scanning the text for information relevant to the focus of the question.

Carefully read the following article twice. Use a dictionary to find the meanings of any unknown vocabulary in the extract.

This article is taken from *Moranifesto* by Caitlin Moran, a collection of her articles written for *The Times* newspaper and published in 2016. In this article, she talks about her decision to give up wearing high heels in favour of more comfortable shoes and clothing.

Source A

'I have given up heels. Like, totally'

I came to a decision last week that, frankly, I'm surprised I didn't make years ago: I've given up on high heels.

I thought I had no option, you see. If you're going to a black-tie event, that means wearing a dress – and if you're wearing a
5   dress, you have to wear heels. Smart black cocktail dresses look weird without heels. Most eveningwear looks weird without heels. You *could* boldly wear trainers, like Lily Allen in 2005 – but that seems too contrary. You're not trying to make a massive style statement. You just want to look *normal*, and nice. Appropriate.

10   And so you put on the Blisteze pads, and the heels, and the dress, and pay the cab fare, and don't dance, and gradually slump in pain, and then – if you're me – fall down a flight of stairs and break three ribs, and think, 'You know what – balls to this. I'm tired of being scared of stairs, and spending every important event I go to worried
15   I'll fall over and show my knickers. I'm going to do what *men* do.'

For when men go to evening events, they can run upstairs, and dance, and get the Tube there and back, thus saving £50 – because they wear a suit, and some nice shoes, which they might have polished; but that is pretty much the extent of their primping.
20   They are safe and comfortable and happier and better off, simply because they are not wearing a short tight dress and a pair of heels.

At the last two events I went to – award ceremonies, black tie – I did as men to. I wore a suit. A tuxedo jacket, shorts, a silk blouse, and flat shoes: flat green-and-gold brogues from Marni, that I
25   can walk to the Tube in, and dance in, and stand in with perfect posture, enjoying my evening.

And it felt *amazing* – to be able to walk around with my hands in my pocket, whistling. To feel *ease*. To know I need never feel anxious about what to wear to a posh event again – I've got my outfit, and
30   my shoes, and I don't really need to think about them again for the next five years – unless it's to go wild, and maybe buy a new blouse.

I felt like I'd discovered an astonishing secret.

So, yes. I have finally given up heels. And it is just jim-dandy.

Activity 4

Answer the questions below related to Source A.

a. List three things that Moran feels high heels prevent her from doing.

----

b. Why does Moran wear high heels in the first place?

----

c. What is Moran's solution to wearing high heels?

----

d. What is Moran's overall **tone** in the text?

Activity 5

In order to succeed with Question 4, you first need to use your skills of deduction to understand the writer's perspective.

a. One of Moran's ideas has been annotated in the extract below. Scan the extract and highlight two more pieces of evidence that show her perspective on clothing. Consider:

- How does she feel about high heels?
- What are her concerns or ideas?
- How does she approach the issue?

b. Now scan the rest of the text and highlight any additional evidence that shows her perspective on clothing.

Key term

tone: manner of expression that shows the writer's attitude, for example, a humorous, sarcastic or angry tone

I thought I had no option, you see. If you're going to a black-tie event, that means wearing a dress – and if you're wearing a dress, you have to wear heels. Smart black cocktail dresses look weird without heels. Most eveningwear looks weird without heels.
5   You *could* boldly wear trainers, like Lily Allen in 2005 – but that seems too contrary. You're not trying to make a massive style statement. You just want to look *normal*, and nice. Appropriate.

She considers her position to be inevitable.

10 And so you put on the Blisteze pads, and the heels, and the dress, and pay the cab fare, and don't dance, and gradually slump in pain, and then – if you're me – fall down a flight of stairs and break three ribs, and think, 'You know what – balls to this. I'm tired of being scared of stairs, and spending every important event I go to worried I'll fall over and show my knickers. I'm going to do what *men* do.'

Activity 6

You need to select a range of judicious quotations – that is, choosing quotations that show good sense and judgement. To do this, review the quotations you've highlighted and write out the four most relevant ones.

1. _____

_____

2. _____

_____

3. _____

_____

4. _____

_____

Writing your response

Activity 7

a. Look at the two exemplar responses below. Using different-coloured pens or highlighters, identify in each response where you can see the:

- statement
- quotation(s)
- inference(s).

Student A

At the start of the text Moran feels as if she has no choice but to wear high heels despite being afraid of the consequences. We see this when we learn that she is 'scared of stairs' while wearing high heels, suggesting that her choice of footwear has an impact on her both physically and mentally.

Student B

At the start of the text Moran feels as if she has no choice but to wear high heels despite falling 'down a flight of stairs' and constantly being 'worried' about the consequences. It suggests she is not happy or comfortable wearing high heels, and implies that the impact that wearing high heels has had on her is far greater than discomfort: heels have caused her both physical pain and anxiety.

Upgrade

Using Statement, Quotation, Inference (SQI) to approach the 'what' element of the question will help you to organise your response and hit the 'what' bullet points on the mark scheme ladder.

Activity 7 *continued*

b. Which response shows Level 3 qualities and which shows Level 4 qualities? What extra skill can you see in the Level 4-style response?

Activity 8

Answer the following question using the Statement, Quotation, Inference approach. You could use some of the sentence starters below if you wish.

Example Exam Question

4 What are the writer of Source A's views and perspective on clothing?

You should:

- make a strong statement that links directly with the focus of the question
- support this statement with a well-chosen quotation (preferably embedded)
- show your understanding by making subtle and finely judged inferences.

Sentence starters:

The writer thinks that...

The writer seems to feel that...

The writer's view is that...

The writer is trying to show us that...

The writer experiences a feeling of...

The writer takes the viewpoint that...

The writer seems to believe that...

Comparing perspectives

The most challenging part of Question 4 is that you have to compare the perspectives of two writers. This means you need to apply your inference skills to more than one text. Remember: the second text will always be 19th-century non-fiction.

Read the journal extract opposite twice. It was written in the 19th century and so you may find there are parts that are harder to understand, therefore take your time and remember to use the glossary to help you.

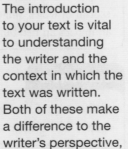

Upgrade

The introduction to your text is vital to understanding the writer and the context in which the text was written. Both of these make a difference to the writer's perspective, so don't ignore the introduction.

This journal extract is taken from *Improperly Dressed* by Ralph David Blumenfeld and was published in 1890. In it the writer describes being 'improperly dressed' when attending a meeting with the Governor of the Bank of England.

Source B

Improperly Dressed by Ralph David Blumenfeld

Unfortunately I was what was called 'improperly dressed'. I have not conformed to the rule that in order to have the *entrée* in the City one must wear a silk hat and a **frock coat**. I have been disporting myself in a bowler hat and tweeds,
5   while I still further **transgress** by wearing light flannel shirts instead of white linen. It is something of a fad to be wearing these loose garments, but I am pleasing myself, and not Dame Fashion. I frequently notice that my loose-fronted shirt is the object of comment among people, who think that one
10   is uncivilised unless the manly bosom is adorned with a stiff white shirt.

So I presented myself at the Bank and, handing in my **card**, asked to see the Governor, Mr Lidderdale. A **functionary** in a frock coat, who took my card, scrutinised
15   me suspiciously, **boggled** at my tweed suit and brown shoes and my outrageous shirt, and then turned on his heel to fetch a colleague, also in a frock coat. He, too, looked puzzled, but I insisted, and finally they took my card.

Glossary

entrée: the right to enter a place or to join a particular group

frock coat: a long, double-breasted coat for men

transgress: break a rule or law

card: business card

functionary: an official

boggled: looked amazed or puzzled

🖉 **Activity 9**

What inferences can you make from Source B? Answer the following questions.

a. What clothing does Blumenfeld prefer to wear?

- -

b. What is his opinion of the clothing worn by most other men in the City?

- -

c. What does he suspect others think of his choice of clothing?

- -

Activity 10

Just as in Source A, you need to understand the writer's perspective on the focus of the question.

a. Read Source B again, highlighting and annotating evidence that shows the writer's perspective on clothing. Consider the following questions.

- How does he feel about clothing?
- What is his idea about the clothing of others?
- How does he approach the issue of acceptable dress?

b. Scan the quotations you have highlighted and write out the four or five most relevant ones.

1. _____

2. _____

3. _____

4. _____

5. _____

c. Now answer this question using the Statement, Quotation, Inference approach.

> **Example Exam Question**
>
> **4** What are the writer of Source B's views and perspective on clothing?

_____

_____

_____

_____

_____

Try it with support

Once you have read through both source texts and worked out both writers' perspectives, you might find it helpful to organise your findings in a table in order to compare the texts and plan your response.

> **Upgrade**
>
> Although Paper 2 Question 4 asks you to 'compare', you should look for comparisons (similarities) *and* contrasts (differences) in the perspectives presented.

Activity 11

a. Complete the table, following the instructions below to also add two perspectives of your own.

1. Look over your notes on Sources A and B so far. Select perspectives, ideas and feelings that are present in both texts, listing them in the first column of your table.

2. Note down what each writer thinks, embedding a quotation that backs up each of your points.

Perspective	Explain Source A	Explain Source B
Social expectation or etiquette	Moran initially believes she has to wear high heels to 'important events' but later dismisses this idea.	Blumenfeld is 'pleasing himself', placing his own comfort ahead of social etiquette.
Comfort		

b. Use the ideas in your table to write two short paragraphs comparing both writers' ideas and perspectives on clothing.

Example Exam Question

4 For this question, you need to refer to the **whole of Source A**, together with the **whole of Source B**.

Compare the writers' views and perspectives on clothing.

Unit 2: Analysing the writers' methods and their effects (Paper 2 Question 4)

Understand it

As in the source text for Paper 1 Question 4, the methods the writers use to get across their perspectives in Sources A and B are important. You must not treat Paper 2 Question 4 simply as a comparison of language or you will miss out two of the four bullet points on the mark scheme.

You have dealt with the 'what' (highlighted yellow below) and now you are going to tackle the 'how' elements (green) of the mark scheme.

Learning focus:

- Recognise and select language and structural features in a text.
- Give a judicious range of examples.
- Comment perceptively and in detail on the effects of those features.

Level 4	
Perceptive, detailed comparison	• Compares ideas and perspectives in a perceptive way
	• Analyses how writers' methods are used
13–16 marks	• Selects a range of judicious supporting detail from both texts
	• Shows a detailed understanding of the different ideas and perspectives in both texts

Activity 1

Remind yourself what is meant by the term 'writers' methods'.

a. Complete the table below, giving a definition and example of each method, then add two methods of your own. Revisit earlier units of this workbook or use a dictionary if you need to.

b. Label each method to show if it is 'language', 'structure' or 'both'.

Method	Definition	Example
Metaphor		
Direct address		
Juxtaposition		

Activity 1 *continued*

Humour		
Hyperbole		
Declarative sentence		
Semantic field		

Revise it

Think about the following question, then carefully read Source A on the next page twice.

Example Exam Question

> **4** How do the writer's methods show his thoughts, feelings and perspectives about his surroundings?

This restaurant review was written for *The Guardian* newspaper by Jay Rayner in 2016. The reviewer is sampling the food at a small fish restaurant near Newcastle. This is the start of his article.

Source A

'Riley's fish shack, Tynemouth: restaurant review' by Jay Rayner

Jay is in love, and he doesn't care who knows it. The object of his desire? A pair of shipping containers half an hour's drive from Newcastle…

5 Call off the search. Close down the web browser and put away the guide books. I have found the eating experience of the year. It's the sort of place that people mumble irritatingly about to each other, in a way that makes it sound like some tiresome gastronomic **Shangri-La**; honey-toned and utterly unobtainable. We roll our eyes at such stories. We assume that the experience

10 is better in the retelling than in the reality, its virtues amplified by the efforts some might have to make to get there. Lunch always tastes better when it comes glazed with struggle.

Glossary

Shangri-La: a fictional mystical place

Activity 2

Select three quotations from the highlighted words and phrases in Source A. Then, using the prompts below to help you, complete the table.

- What method has the writer used?

- How does this feature link to or emphasise the writer's perspective?

- What does this feature make me think, feel or imagine?

- What is this structural feature doing or adding to my interpretation of the text?

- Why has the writer included or chosen this feature?

Quotation	Methods the writer uses to show his thoughts/feelings/perspectives about his surroundings
'I have found the eating experience of the year'	Declarative sentence. He is clear and convincing in his feelings towards this restaurant.

Activity 2 *continued*

Activity 3

a. Read the next paragraph from Rayner's review on the next page. Highlight and annotate other methods that he uses to express his thoughts and perspective on his surroundings.

b. Select the best three methods, then expand on them in the table below.

Quotation	Methods the writer uses to show his thoughts/ feelings/perspectives about his surroundings

Source A

'Riley's fish shack, Tynemouth: restaurant review' by Jay Rayner

To be fair some of this may apply to Riley's Fish Shack. It's on the beach at King Edward's Bay, half an hour's drive from Newcastle. It really is hidden. The sat nav took me to a shopping street in Tynemouth. We parked up and wandered to the front. There, we
5 looked down over the Edwardian railings and the **vertiginous** shoreline to the shack. We knew it was the place. There was a film-fun-style cartoon of a fish skeleton on the roof, the motif repeated across all the deckchairs out front. A wisp of smoke **pirouetted** from its Hobbit chimney on the roof. We started our descent.

10 This is a **Boden** photoshoot brought to life. It is every boho, middle-class food fantasy made real. And it's fantastic!

Glossary

vertiginous: extremely high or steep

pirouette: ballet term for a spin on one foot

Boden: a clothing company

Upgrade

Annotating your highlighting helps you gather and make notes on your thoughts. It also helps you spot patterns in the writing and makes planning easier.

Activity 4

a. Select two of your quotations from the tables in Activities 2 and/or 3. Write a short paragraph for each quotation, analysing the writer's methods. Remember to link your analysis to the question.

Example Exam Question

4 How do the writer's methods show his thoughts, feelings and perspectives about his surroundings?

You should:

- clearly identify a language or structural feature by using the correct terminology
- give precise examples of that feature
- write up your comment on effects from your notes, considering what the feature makes you think, feel or imagine.

Activity 4 *continued*

Activity 5

a. Read the student response below and make notes on how they have hit Level 4.

b. Look back at your own response and try to highlight where you have met the mark scheme. If you need to, try to improve your response on a separate piece of paper.

Upgrade

Look back at your responses in Units 1 and 2 if you need to recap on analysing language and/or structure.

> Selects a range of judicious supporting detail

> Analyses how writer's methods are used

The writer uses the semantic field of fantasy to create a sense of mystery around the restaurant and his surroundings, which emphasises his enjoyment of the experience. The personification of the smoke that 'pirouetted', alongside the reference to 'Hobbit' and 'Shangri-La' conjures an image of a far-away land, something not of this world. This effect is further developed with the use of the short sentence, 'We started our descent', creating the image of him going on an adventure that will take him far away from his starting point. All of this combines to create a sense of mystery; it is not just a meal at a restaurant but an exploration.

Unit 3: Planning and writing a complete critical comparison (Paper 2 Question 4)

Understand it

As you saw in Unit 1, the key point for Paper 2 Question 4 is that it is about the writers' thoughts, feelings, perspectives and experiences – not just about the content of the texts. You should be 'inside' the text looking out!

Thinking about the context of a text

In order to do this successfully, it's important that you take time to consider the context in which the writing took place. The context will often affect a writer's feelings and perspectives on the topic they are writing about. For example, someone writing about a family holiday will do so more honestly and intimately in a letter to a sister or brother than they will if writing an article for a national newspaper.

Activity 1

Look at the introduction to Source A below and how it has been annotated. Then annotate the introduction to Source B.

Learning focus:
- Respond to Paper 2 Question 4 in a detailed way.
- Bring together the 'what' and 'how' elements of the question in a perceptive way.

Upgrade

Taking the time to engage with the context of the text will mean you have a clearer idea about the writer's perspectives before you start reading the main text.

Source A

Improperly Dressed
by Ralph David Blumenfeld

In this journal extract from 1890, the writer describes being 'improperly dressed' when attending a meeting with the Governor of the Bank of England.

> Form: usually personal notes

> 19th century when social etiquette was more important

> Describes personal experience

Source B

'I have given up heels. Like, totally'
by Caitlin Moran

This article is taken from *Moranifesto* by Caitlin Moran. *Moranifesto* is a collection of articles written for *The Times* newspaper. In this article, Moran talks about her decision to give up wearing high heels.

Comparing texts

Another key ingredient to a successful response to Paper 2 Question 4 is your ability to cross-compare the texts. This means that each paragraph in your response weaves in both texts to make comparative points relating to the focus of the question. This will help you to avoid writing all about one text, then all about the other.

Activity 2

Look at the plans below. In which plan are the texts cross-compared?

Example Exam Question

> **4** Compare how the writers convey their views and perspectives on their pets.

Plan A	Source A	Source B
Paragraph 1	Loves dogs	
Paragraph 2	Why dogs make good pets	
Paragraph 3		Loves cats
Paragraph 4		Why cats make good pets

Plan B	Source A	Source B
Paragraph 1	Loves dogs	Loves cats
Paragraph 2	Why dogs make good pets	Why cats make good pets
Paragraph 3	Dogs hate to be left alone	Cats wander off for days at a time
Paragraph 4	Dogs cost a lot of money	Cats are inexpensive pets

The activities you have just completed will help you hit Level 4 in the mark scheme.

Level 4	• Compares ideas and perspectives in a perceptive way
Perceptive, detailed comparison	• Analyses how writers' methods are used
13–16 marks	• Selects a range of judicious supporting detail from both texts
	• Shows a detailed understanding of the different ideas and perspectives in both texts

Revise it

To be successful with Paper 2 Question 4, it's important to plan. Look at the following example exam question, then carefully read Source A twice, and complete Activity 3.

4 For this question, you need to refer to the **whole of Source A**, together with the **whole of Source B**.

Compare how the writers convey their different perspectives on school and childhood.

In your answer, you could:

- compare their different perspectives
- compare the methods the writers use to convey their different perspectives
- support your response with references to both texts.

[16 marks]

Upgrade

Remember to get into the habit of highlighting the focus of the question.

This extract is taken from a collection of memoirs looking back at growing up in the north-east of England in the 1930s. In this extract, a woman reflects on her time at school during the Second World War.

Source A

A Young Girl's School Memories

I commenced school in 1939 at the Bewicke Infants, which was situated on Tynemouth Road. Sadly, it is no longer there having been demolished some years ago and the site is now a Health Centre.

5   As the Second World War commenced that year, our school was taken over by the ARP (Air-Raid Wardens). Their job was to distribute gas masks to everyone in case the Germans used deadly gas, which fortunately, they did not. We were all transferred to Stephenson
10 Memorial School, which had to accommodate infants, juniors and senior pupils.

Air-Raid shelters were built down the right-hand side of the playground, which shut in the light from the classrooms, making them dark as night, even on the
15 brightest summer day. When a warning siren was given all pupils had to file into the shelters. We would sing merry songs and recite poetry so as not to be too frightened. If you wanted to go to the toilet whilst in the shelters you had to go outside the door and squat over
20 a bucket. You were not allowed to leave the shelter until the all-clear had sounded, or you might have been killed!

We had assembly every morning, said our prayers and sang hymns for half an hour. We were taught science, maths, English, geography, history, art, domestic
25   science, needlework and PE. Although we had very little equipment for PE – I think a netball and posts and **shintey** stick and goal nets were all we had.

A Miss Cooke was the headmistress then and there was only one married teacher, a Mrs Hutchinson, who took
30   us for needlework, the rest were all single women.

When you went into the senior class you were given teams, e.g. Austen, Brontë, Cavelle and Darling, the teams all named after famous women. Each team had a colour, Austen was red, Brontë was green, Cavelle was
35   yellow and Darling was blue. I chose to be in Cavelle team and you remained with that team until you left school. There was great rivalry between the teams, as you got a shield at the end of term for the best. Cavelle always seemed to win and I was very proud.

40   At Christmas-time we would hold a concert in the school hall. Anyone with a good voice or who could recite would get up on the stage and do their stuff. We once did a play of 'Alice in Wonderland' and I got the part of the Dormouse.

45   Even though conditions were very bad due to the war, food was rationed and school dinners were always the same, corned beef, potatoes and plenty of cabbage. We did get milk every morning and afternoon and gleefully looked forward to it. Sometimes the Education Authority
50   would visit the school and measure our feet. If you had no shoes, as was the case for many children, they would provide laced-up boots, which were hated.

Teachers had a very difficult time, but gave us a marvellous education. I must add that the discipline was
55   very high and the belt was used often if you misbehaved or were late three times in a week. I was once given ten belts, five on each hand for having ten spelling mistakes out of twenty given. We took it all as a matter of course and it did not do us any harm.

> Food unappetising and repetitive

> Adjective: something so simple gave great pleasure

Glossary

shintey a game with similarities to hockey or lacrosse

Activity 3

a. Before you start planning, take time to step back and consider this writer's perspectives.

1. What is her point of view?

----

2. What issues did she face?

----

3. How does she feel about her childhood and school life?

----

b. Highlight five or six quotations in the source that give you a clear indication of the writer's feelings, thoughts and point of view about school and childhood. Add notes on your ideas and inferences next to each quotation.

c. In a different colour, highlight three or four examples of language or structure that show the writer's perspective. Add notes on your ideas and inferences next to each quotation.

Read Source B carefully twice, then complete Activity 4.

Ragged Schools were set up to provide free education for poor and deprived children. This extract is taken from a fundraising pamphlet published in 1853 aimed at raising money for Ragged Schools.

Source B

A Letter about Ragged Schools

There are hundreds of poor children who have either no home to go to, or such an one as you would fear to enter; that many pass the night under arches, or on the steps of doors, or wherever they can – poor unhappy
5   little beings! Oh! When you pray for yourselves, and ask God to bless your father and mother, your brothers and sisters, then do not forget to ask Him also to help the poor outcasts.

Now, Ragged Schools have been set on foot by kind
10   and Christian people on purpose to do good to these unhappy children. They are brought to these schools, and there they have their torn, dirty clothes taken off,

and after being washed, and made nice and clean, they have others put on to wear all day, but at night they are
15 obliged to have their dirty ones put on again, because their parents are so wicked, that if they went home in good clothes they would take them from them and sell them, and spend the money on something to drink. Then they would send the children out again in miserable and
20 filthy rags, or nearly without clothes at all; so the kind people at the schools take care of the clean clothing for them at night. The children stay at school all day and have food provided for them. Sometimes they have one thing, sometimes another.

25 The day I was at Dr Guthrie's school, they had each a basin of nice hot soup and a good-sized piece of bread. What a treat for these poor, neglected, hungry things! Perhaps you, my young friends, never knew what it was to want a morsel of bread. It is a terrible thing to be very
30 hungry and to have nothing to eat; a terrible thing to see the shop windows full of nice bread, and cakes, etc.; to be very, very hungry, and to have no means of obtaining anything but by stealing.

> Bread and soup is their only meal.

> The most basic meal is a 'treat'.

> Use of 'things' shows their 'worth'.

> Emphasises how hungry and poor they are

Activity 4

a. Before you start planning, take time to step back and consider this writer's perspectives.

   1. What is the writer's point of view?

   ----

   2. What issues do the children the writer talks about face?

   ----

   3. How does the writer feel about childhood and school life?

   ----

b. Highlight five or six quotations in the source that give you a clear indication of the writer's feelings, thoughts and point of view about school and childhood. Add notes on your ideas and inferences next to each quotation.

c. In a different colour, highlight three or four examples of language or structure that show the writer's perspective. Add notes on your ideas and inferences next to each quotation.

Activity 5

Select your best notes and create a plan on a separate sheet of paper, using the headings in the table below. Remember that to compare and contrast you have to write about the differences and similarities in the texts. You could use some of the phrases below to help make comparisons.

similarly   in comparison   likewise   whereas   in contrast   unlike

Select four perspectives from Source A.	Select four perspectives from Source B.
<ul><li></li><li></li><li></li><li></li></ul>	<ul><li></li><li></li><li></li><li></li></ul>
Select two writers' methods from Source A used to show their thoughts/feelings/perspectives.	**Select two writers' methods from Source B used to show their thoughts/feelings/perspectives.**
<ul><li></li><li></li></ul>	<ul><li></li><li></li></ul>

Now that you have made notes about each writer's perspectives and the methods they used, you are going to pull together 'what' their perspectives are and 'how' they present them.

Activity 6

a. Look at the student response below and take note of how and where they have met the mark scheme.

> Both writers discuss the hardships of school life. Source A explains that 'conditions were very bad' and the food they were given never varied from 'corned beef, potatoes and plenty of cabbage', highlighting one of the main issues facing school children at the time and suggesting that the food and the repetition of the same meal wasn't something the writer took pleasure in. However, the writer 'gleefully' received her daily milk. The use of this childish adjective emphasises how excited she was about something very simple and further illustrates that life was so hard that a drink of milk could bring such pleasure. Similarly, in Source B...

Upgrade

If you manage to add all the elements shown in the paragraph opposite, you will have a full comparative paragraph. In the exam, you should aim to write at least four paragraphs like this for Paper 2 Question 4.

Level 4	• Compares ideas and perspectives in a perceptive way
Perceptive, detailed comparison	• Analyses how writers' methods are used
13–16 marks	• Selects a range of judicious supporting detail from both texts
	• Shows a detailed understanding of the different ideas and perspectives in both texts

b. On a separate piece of paper, complete the paragraph using your highlighted quotations from Source B.

c. Complete your response to the question by writing another three similar paragraphs.

Try it with support

You are now going to tackle a full Paper 2 Question 4.

Activity 7

Read the question and highlight the focus.

Example Exam Question

4 For this question, you need to refer to the **whole of Source A**, together with the **whole of Source B**.

Compare how the writers convey their different perspectives on the exhibitions they visit.

In your answer, you could:

- compare their different perspectives

- compare the methods the writers use to convey their different perspectives

- support your response with references to both texts.

[16 marks]

Activity 8

a. Read the introduction to Source A below and note what it tells you about the writer and the text. Are there any clues to the writer's perspective?

b. Read Source A on page 96 carefully twice. Highlight or underline five or six examples of the writer's perspective on her surroundings and any interesting words, phrases or language features that she uses to describe her surroundings.

c. Annotate your selected examples with comments on the writer's perspectives to help you plan your response to the question.

d. Comment on the writer's methods in the same way, focusing on what she wants you to think, feel and/or imagine. Consider how you respond to the writing.

This article about the Design Museum, London is taken from *Time Out* magazine, 2018. Having visited the museum, the journalist is giving her opinion and review of the latest exhibition.

Source A

'Home futures' by Rosemary Waugh

William Morris famously advised: 'have nothing in your houses that you do not know to be useful or believe to be beautiful'. The Design Museum's latest exhibition is filled with over 150 domestic designs both useful and beautiful, all created with the intention of
5 revolutionising how we conduct ourselves behind closed doors.

The medium-sized show is split into six sections: 'living smart', 'living on the move', 'living autonomously', 'living with less', 'living with others' and 'domestic **arcadia**'. The interesting bit is that the exhibits were all designed at any point from 1950 onwards, with
10 more on display from the past than the present. So the end product is a show that's more focused on what people hoped the future would hold than what it necessarily did.

There's a bit of everything included here, from dream-big plans for entire new homes, to dream-small inventions of new table lamps. Some
15 of it's brilliant, some of it's bonkers and some is just flat-out confusing.

Highlights include micro-environment shower and toilet pods (useful); contemporary tapestries featuring modern appliances (beautiful); a multi-functional '70s **kaftan** capable of transforming into other garments (useful); frequent use of pastel pinks, space-
20 age white and happiness-inducing orange (beautiful); and an inflatable pod to live in (vaguely useful, especially for anyone wanting more personal space on the tube).

But the best part is 'domestic arcadia', a room filled with lumpy, bumpy, generally odd-looking soft furnishings – because who hasn't
25 found themselves in need of an armchair made entirely of oversized foam grass, or a sofa in the shape of a massive bird's nest? The best part is that you're invited to try them all out, making the final room the adult gallery visitor's equivalent of a soft play area.

In the interest of writing a fair review, I treated my creaking, desk-
30 sore body to a rest on all of them and discovered that a silver mass of chain-link metal and bent poles (imagine the most **ergonomic** children's playground equipment possible) is INCREDIBLY COMFORTABLE. Like lying on a cool, metallic cloud gently cradling each knotty, contorted muscle, while angels pluck harp strings and
35 sing lullabies about how beautiful you are. Designed by SO-IL, it's ugly and useless. But I really, really want one.

Glossary

arcadia: an idea of the perfect place

kaftan: a long tunic or loose dress

ergonomic: designed for efficiency and comfort

Activity 9

a. Read the introduction to Source B and note what it tells you about the writer and the text. Are there any clues to the writer's perspective?

b. Now complete parts b–d in Activity 8 for Source B, as you did for Source A. This time consider whether the perspective and methods are the same or different to those in Source A. Are there any shared points of view, feelings or ideas that you can base your response on? Use a comparison table if it helps you.

In this letter of 1851, writer Charlotte Brontë describes to her father her second visit to the Great Exhibition at the Crystal Palace in London. The Great Exhibition was visited by millions of people, who would have seen inventions and manufactured goods from Britain as well as from other countries.

Source B

Letter from Charlotte Brontë to her father

Dear Papa, – I was very glad to hear that you continued in pretty good health, and that Mr. Cartman came to help you on Sunday. I fear you will not have had a very comfortable week in the dining-room; but by this time I suppose the parlour reformation will be
5 nearly completed, and you will soon be able to return to your own quarters. The letter you sent me this morning was from Mary Taylor. She continues well and happy in New Zealand, and her shop seems to answer well.
The French newspaper duly arrived. Yesterday I went for the
10 second time to the Crystal Palace. We remained in it about three hours, and I must say I was more struck with it on this occasion than at my first visit, it is a wonderful place – vast, strange, new, and impossible to describe. Its grandeur does not consist in *one* thing, but in the assemblage of *all* things. Whatever human
15 industry has created, you find there, from the great compartments filled with railway engines and boilers, with mill machinery in full work, with splendid carriages of all kinds, with harness of every description – to the glass covered and velvet spread stands loaded with the most gorgeous work of the **goldsmith and**
20 **silversmith**, and the carefully guarded caskets full of real diamonds, and pearls worth hundreds of thousands of pounds. It may be called a **bazaar** or a fair, but it is such a bazaar or fair as Eastern **genii** might have created. It seems as if only magic could have gathered this mass of wealth from all ends of the earth – as if
25 none but supernatural hands could have arranged this, with such blaze and contrast of colours and marvellous power of effect. The multitude filling the great aisles seems ruled and subdued by some invisible influence. Amongst the thirty thousand souls that peopled it the day I was there not one loud noise was to be heard, not one

97

30   irregular movement seen; the living tide rolls on quietly, with a deep
     hum like the sea heard from the distance.

     I hope, dear papa, that you, Mr. Nicholls, and all at home continue
     well. Tell Martha to take her scrubbing and cleaning in moderation
     and not overwork herself. With kind regards to her and Tabby, –

35   I am, your affectionate daughter,

     C Brontë.

Glossary

goldsmith and silversmith:
   craftspeople who work with gold
   and silver
bazaar: market

genii: plural of genie; a supernatural
   being from Arabian folklore, often
   trapped in a bottle or oil lamp, who
   can grant wishes

Activity 10

a. Select the best four examples of each writer's perspective and the
methods they use to get these across.

b. Write your response to the example exam question on a separate sheet
of paper. You should aim to write four paragraphs. To hit all
aspects of the Level 4 mark scheme, in each paragraph you should:

- make a precise and definite comparison of the writers' perspectives in
  relation to the focus

- use well-chosen quotations to support your points

- show your understanding by making a thoughtful, perceptive inference

- identify a language or structural feature

- give the example of it precisely and judiciously

- analyse the effect in detail, developing your ideas.

Example Exam Question

4 For this question, you need to refer to the **whole of Source A**,
together with the **whole of Source B**.

Compare how the writers convey their different perspectives on
the exhibitions they visit.

In your answer, you could:

- compare their different perspectives

- compare the methods the writers use to convey their different
  perspectives

- support your response with references to both texts.

[16 marks]

Upgrade

Remember to use comparative language in your response and to comment on both of the writers' perspectives. Use the sentence starters below to help you.

Sentence starters

The writer thinks that...

The writer seems to feel that...

The writer's view is that...

The writer is trying to show us that...

The writer experiences a feeling of...

The writer takes the viewpoint that...

The writer seems to believe that...

Progress check

	I'm confident	I need more practice	I'm not confident
I can compare ideas and perspectives in a detailed and thoughtful way.			
I can analyse the writers' methods.			
I can select a judicious range of textual detail from both texts.			
I can show a detailed and perceptive understanding of the different ideas and perspectives in both texts.			

Sample exam paper 1

Source A:

This is an extract from the novel The Stars Are Fire *by Anita Shreve. In this extract, Grace is at home with her children while her husband is helping to fight a wildfire after a drought that summer.*

Grace has set aside a pile of belongings on the floor of the living room. Clothes, baby food, canned milk, a few photographs, two of Gene's most prized surveying antiques, all the important papers in the drawer of the living room desk, blankets, several bottles of water. How will she manage to get the provisions out of the house with two children in tow is an unsolved problem. Gene took the car this morning, stating that he was going to help other men create a   5 firebreak to stop the wildfire from nearing Hunts Beach. She wishes he would come home.

Grace brings the supplies out to the back porch to be closer to the car when Gene comes for them. Something that looks like a bat skims the screen and startles Grace. But its flight is too slow and too close to the ground to be a bat. It seems to float to the sunburned glass and stay there, weightless. With caution, she opens the door to get a better look and as she does, an   10 insect flutters against her cheek. She slaps the bug away and watches the pieces drift to the ground. Not a bat, not a bug. Fragments of burned paper, carried on the wind.

Grace floats like a paper fragment into her house and up the stairs to where her children sleep. In a slow dance of exhaustion and relief, she slips into her summer nightgown and lies back on her pillow. She ought to stay awake and watch over her house and her children in case the   15 wind switches direction. She ought to go downstairs and wait in the kitchen for Gene. Will he be covered in soot, desperate for a glass of water? But won't the east wind have reached the men by now, signalling a few hours to go home and get some sleep?

She rolls over to put her cheek to the pillow. She will take a catnap and be refreshed and ready for whatever comes next.   20

Hot breath on Grace's face. Claire is screaming, and Grace is on her feet. As she lifts her daughter, a wall of fire fills the window. Perhaps a quarter of a mile back, if even that. Where's Gene? Didn't he come home? She picks Tom up from his crib and feels a wet diaper. No time to change him.

She scurries down the stairs carrying both children. She deposits them in the carriage in the   25 hallway and pushes it onto the screened porch. Claire begins to cough in the smoky air. […]

She stuffs blankets, diapers, baby food, and water into the carriage behind the children. She loops the kids' clothes around the upper bits of metal and ties them in knots. She'll have to leave the mementoes.

As she manoeuvres the vehicle to the edge of the grass, a bomb goes off, the explosion one   30 Grace can feel right through her feet and legs. The children are silent, as if awed by the sound.

"A fuel tank in a house on Seventh Street," she hears one man shout to another.

Sparks and embers swirl around Grace. There's chaos in the streets. She hears cars moving, women screaming. Balls of flame seem to leap from treetop to treetop, giving the fire a frightening momentum. A tree catches fire at the top, and the fire races down the trunk and   35 into a house below. Another bomb. The fire turns tree after tree into tall torches.

Fields resemble hot coals. For as far as she can see, there's an unbroken line of fire. Cars are travelling, but where can they go?

An ember lands on the hood of the carriage. Grace swipes it off and begins to run. Heat and common sense push her to the seawall. A deer leaps across the street with her, chased by the freight train bearing down on all of them. 40

She takes the children from the carriage and sets them on a blanket on the sand. On another blanket, she lays out what provisions she has brought. Abandoning the carriage, she begins to drag both blankets away from the fire and closer to the water. When the sand feels wet underfoot, she stops. 45

Section A: Reading

01   Reread the first part of the source from lines 1-5. List four things Grace is collecting.

[4 marks]

02   Look in detail at the section below.

Grace brings the supplies out to the back porch to be closer to the car when Gene comes for them. Something that looks like a bat skims the screen and startles Grace. But its flight is too slow and too close to the ground to be a bat. It seems to float to the sunburned glass and stay there, weightless. With caution, she opens the door to get a better look and as she does, an insect flutters against her cheek. She slaps the bug away and watches the pieces drift to the ground. Not a bat, not a bug. Fragments of burned paper, carried on the wind.

Grace floats like a paper fragment into her house and up the stairs to where her children sleep. In a slow dance of exhaustion and relief, she slips into her summer nightgown and lies back on her pillow. She ought to stay awake and watch over her house and her children in case the wind switches direction. She ought to go downstairs and wait in the kitchen for Gene. Will he be covered in soot, desperate for a glass of water? But won't the east wind have reached the men by now, signalling a few hours to go home and get some sleep?

How does the writer use language here to describe Grace's actions and thoughts?

You could include the writer's choice of:

* words and phrases
* language features and techniques
* sentence forms.

[8 marks]

03   You now need to think about the whole of the source.

This text is an extract from a novel. How has the writer structured the text to interest you as a reader?

You could write about:

* what the writer focuses your attention on at the beginning
* how and why the writer changes the focus as the source develops
* any other structural features that interest you.

[8 marks]

04   Focus your answer on the second part of the source, from 'Hot breath on Grace's face.' to the end.

A student, having read this part of the text, said: 'The writer here creates a real sense of tension and shows Grace's panic.' To what extent do you agree?

In your response you could:

* consider your own impressions of the situation and Grace's response
* evaluate how the writer creates that impression and response
* support your opinions with quotations from the text.

[20 marks]

Section B: Writing

You are advised to spend 45 minutes on the exam task.

You must write in full sentences.

You are reminded of the need to plan your answers.

You should leave enough time to check your work at the end.

---

0 5   Select one of the tasks below.

Either: Write a description suggested by this picture:

Or:

Write a short story in which a character has to leave a place in a hurry.

(24 marks for content and organisation
16 marks for technical accuracy)
[40 marks]

Sample exam paper 2

Source A:

The Sea Inside by Philip Hoare

This is an extract from a non-fiction book, The Sea Inside, *by Philip Hoare, published in 2013, in which he describes an unusual encounter on a morning swim.*

Winter is a lonely season. That's why I like it. It's easier to be alone; there's no one there to notice. In the silence that ascends and descends at either end of the day, there's room to feel alive. Swimming before dawn, it is so dark I have to leave my bike light on so I can see where I left my clothes. Once the waves washed them clean away, leaving me to wade after them.

The sea doesn't care, it can take or give. Ports are places of grief. In the past, sailors declined   5
to learn to swim, since to be lost overboard – even within sight of the shore – and to fight the waves would only extend the agony. You can only ever be alone out there.

One day, however, with the sea swollen by a near-full moon, I get the feeling I'm not alone. I've just turned back from my farthest point when I'm startled by a sudden *whoosh*. Directly behind me, barely a yard away, is a huge head with shiny dog-like eyes: a large grey seal, fat   10
and full-grown.

I back off, shocked at the sight. I knew there was a seal colony just along the **Solent** – I'd seen grey and harbour seals there, lounging on the mud flats, so blubbery and lazy that algae grew on their backs where they spent all their time basking in the sun, raising their hind flippers in the air to keep them warm on chillier days. From a distance, they look quite cute. But coming   15
face to face with one in the water was another matter. Weighing up to eight hundred pounds, grey seals have sharp claws and teeth that can cause a serious infection, *Mycobacterium marinum*, otherwise known as seal finger, which may result in the loss of the affected digits.

The seal and I regard each other, equally surprised. He's twice my size, clearly a mature male. He raises his grizzly head, lugubriously. I'm not sure what he intends to do, but I'm not going   20
to wait to find out. Kicking out with my feet to persuade the animal to keep its distance, I make for the shore – only to discover that the great beast has followed me, swimming beneath the surface. Scrambling onto the safety of the sea wall and reaching for my clothes, I look down at it.

I was right to be apprehensive. Up close, it is even bigger, almost magnified by the clear   25
water. It looks more like a **manatee** as it hangs there, puffing away quizzically, all whiskers and wrinkles, trying to work out what I am, this pale, unsealish creature. I hurry to dress, keeping one eye on my marine companion. His curiosity satisfied, he turns towards the open water and sets off, popping up at intervals as he works his way upstream, before finally moving out of sight.   30

Glossary: **Solent:** a stretch of the sea off the South Coast of England
manatee: a large sea creature sometimes known as a sea cow

Source B

The Voyage of the Beagle by Charles Darwin

This is an extract from The Voyage of the Beagle *by the naturalist Charles Darwin, published in 1839, which describes his findings on one of the Galapagos Islands, a group of volcanic islands that lie either side of the equator in the Pacific Ocean.*

Considering that these islands are directly under the equator, the climate is far from being excessively hot. This seems to be caused by the low temperature of the surrounding water. Except during one short season, very little rain falls, and even then it is irregular; but the clouds generally hang low. Whilst the lower parts of the islands are very dry, the upper parts, at a height of a thousand feet and upwards, possess a damp climate and a lush vegetation.   5

In the morning of the 17th September we landed on **Chatham Island**, which, like the others, rises with a rounded outline, broken here and there by scattered hillocks, the remains of former craters. Nothing could be less inviting than the first appearance. A broken field of black lava, in the most rugged waves, is covered everywhere by stunted, sunburnt brushwood, which shows little signs of life. The dry and parched surface, being heated by the noonday   10
sun, gave the air a close and sultry feeling, like that from a stove. It seemed even that the bushes smelt unpleasantly.

Although I tried to collect as many plants as possible, I succeeded in getting very few. Such wretched-looking little weeds would have better suited in the arctic rather than near the equator. The brushwood appears, from a short distance, as leafless as our trees during winter;   15
and it was some time before I discovered that not only almost every plant was now in full leaf, but that the greater number were in flower.

Our ship the *Beagle* sailed round Chatham Island, and anchored in several bays. One night I slept on shore on a part of the island where there was an extraordinary number of black truncated cones. From one small rise I counted sixty of them, all topped by craters more or   20
less perfect. The entire surface of this part of the island seems to have been permeated, like a sieve, by **subterranean** vapours. Here and there the lava, whilst soft, has been blown into great bubbles; and in other parts, the tops of caverns have fallen in, leaving circular pits with steep sides. These gave to the country an artificial appearance, which vividly reminded me of those parts of Staffordshire where the great **iron-foundries** are most numerous.   25

The day was glowing hot, and scrambling over the rough surface and through the intricate thickets was very fatiguing; but I was well repaid by the strange scene. As I was walking along I met two large tortoises, each of which must have weighed at least two hundred pounds. One was eating a piece of cactus, and as I approached, it stared at me and slowly walked away; the other gave a deep hiss, and drew in its head. These huge reptiles, surrounded by the black   30
lava, the leafless shrubs, and large cacti, seemed to my fancy like some prehistoric animals. The few dull-coloured birds cared no more for me than they did for the great tortoises.

Glossary: **Chatham Island:** easternmost island in the Galapagos; now more usually called
        by its Spanish name San Cristóbal
     subterranean: under ground or under the surface of the earth
     iron-foundries: factories where metal was melted down to make products.
        They often had many large chimneys.

Section A: Reading

0 1   Look again at **Source A** from lines 1 to 11

Choose four statements below that are TRUE.

Chose a maximum of four statements.

1   The writer likes winter. ⬭

2   The writer does not like to be alone. ⬭

3   It is dark when the writer swims before dawn. ⬭

4   The writer's bike light was washed away. ⬭

5   The writer's clothes were once washed away. ⬭

6   In the past all sailors learned to swim. ⬭

7   The writer meets a baby seal. ⬭

8   The seal is approximately a yard away from the writer. ⬭

[4 marks]

0 2   You need to refer to **Source A** and **Source B** for this question.

Both writers describe an encounter with living creatures.
Use details from both sources to write a summary of the writers' different responses to the creatures they encounter.

[8 marks]

0 3   You now need to refer only to **Source B** from lines 6 to 17. (Para 2 and 3)
How does the writer use language to describe Chatham Island and its vegetation?

[12 marks]

0 4   For this question, you need to refer to the whole of **Source A,** together with the whole of **Source B**.

Compare how the writers convey their different perspectives on the natural world.

In your answer, you could:

• compare their different perspectives on the natural world

• compare the methods the writers use to convey their perspectives

• support your response with references to both texts.

[16 marks]

Section B: Writing

You are advised to spend 45 minutes on the writing task.

You must write in full sentences.

You are reminded of the need to plan your answer.

You should leave enough time to check your work at the end.

0 5 'If we don't act now, we will be unable to save the seas and their creatures from the effects of plastic and pollution.'

Write an article for a newspaper in which you argue your point of view on this statement.

(24 marks for content and organisation
16 marks for technical accuracy)
[40 marks]

Key terms glossary

adjective: a word that describes something named by a noun or pronoun

adverb: a word used to describe verbs, adjectives or other adverbs

alliteration: when the same letter or sound occurs at the beginning of neighbouring words

anaphora: the deliberate repetition of the first part of a sentence or phrase

assonance: repetition of a vowel sound in words close to one another

cohesion: the way a piece of writing links together in terms of vocabulary, phrases, clauses, sentences and paragraphs

cohesive devices: techniques for connecting points, avoiding repetition and signposting arguments

connective: a word that joins phrases or sentences, such as *moreover, as a result, furthermore, in addition, not only... but also, because, therefore, consequently*

connotation: an idea or feeling suggested, in addition to the main meaning

consonance: repetition of a consonant sound in words close to one another

critical evaluation: weighing up and giving an interpretation of the text using your comprehension skills *and* your analytical skills

discourse marker: a word or phrase that helps to manage and organise the flow and structure of writing

evaluate: to assess something and understand its quality

evidence: quotation or direct reference to the text

explicit: stating something openly and exactly

first-person narrative: a story or account told from the point of view of a character or one of the people involved, typically using the pronouns *I* and *we*

flashback: a scene that returns to events in the past

foreshadowing: a sign or hint of something that will happen in the future

fricative: repetition of the consonants 'f', 'v' and 'th'

implicit: not directly stated in the text, but where the meaning is suggested by the information you are given and needs to be inferred or deduced

inferences: sensible conclusions of what is meant by an author, based on clues given in the text

interpret: explain the meaning of something in your own words, showing your understanding

juxtaposition: when things are put next to each other or close together to contrast them

metaphor: a comparison showing the similarity between two quite different things, stating that one actually is the other

modal verb: a type of verb that goes before the main verb, e.g. *will, could, might, should, may, ought*

mood: the feeling or atmosphere created by a piece of writing

motif: a physical or metaphorical item that recurs in a text, taking on a range of meanings

narrative perspective: features that determine what is told and how in a story, including the narrator and/or the character from whose point of view the story is told

narrative voice: the characteristic ways in which the narrator speaks and thinks

noun: a noun identifies a person, place or thing

noun phrase: one or more adjectives with a noun, e.g. *clear + starry + night*

omniscient narrator: a narrator who sees and knows everything

onomatopoeia: the use of words that imitate or suggest what they stand for, e.g. *cuckoo, plop*

pathetic fallacy: giving human feelings to things or animals

personification: giving human qualities or emotions to something that is not human

perspective: someone's point of view or attitude towards something

point of view: opinion, a way of thinking about something

pronoun: a word used to replace a noun, often to avoid repetition

protagonist: the main character in a novel or play

second-person narrative: a story or account told from the point of view of the reader, typically using the pronoun *you*

semantic field: a collection of words with similar meanings or relevant to the same theme

setting: the place or surroundings where an event takes place or something is positioned

sibilance: repetition of soft consonant sounds, such as 's', to create a hissing, hushing or whooshing noise

simile: a comparison showing the similarity between two different things, stating that one is like the other

structure: (noun) the organisation of a text

structure: (verb) organise the text, e.g. by including an introduction, headings, subheadings, lists, and grouping ideas into paragraphs

temporal connective: a word or phrase that tells you when something is happening

tension: the feeling of waiting, as though something is about to happen

third-person narrative: a story or account told by a narrator who is not directly involved, typically using the pronouns *he, she, it* and *they*

tone: manner of expression that shows the writer's attitude, for example, a humorous, sarcastic or angry tone

topic sentence: the sentence that introduces or summarises the main idea in a paragraph

unreliable narrator: a narrator who may not be credible or telling the truth

verb: a word that presents a movement, an action or a feeling, and tells us about when it happened

writer's methods: ways of using linguistic and structural features